I0100091

BUSINESS AHA! TIPS

ON

CREATIVITY

BUSINESS AHA! TIPS
ON
CREATIVITY

Gundars Kaupins
Nancy K. Napier

CC!
PRESS
BOISE STATE
UNIVERSITY

Copyright © 2012 by Gundars Kaupins and Nancy K. Napier

All Rights Reserved
Printed in the United States of America

No part of this publication may be reproduced, stored in or introduced into a retrieval system, or transmitted, in any form, or by any means (electronic, mechanical, photocopying, recording, or otherwise), without the prior permission of the publisher. Request for permission should be directed to ccipress@boisestate.edu, Permission in subject line, or mailed to Permissions, CCI Press, Centre for Creativity and Innovation, Boise State University, 1910 University Drive, Boise, Idaho 83725-1635.

PUBLISHED BY CCI PRESS
of Boise State University

Managing editor: Stephanie Chism
Production Manager: Joanna Lui
Contributions by Bianca Jochimsen
Cover design by Paul Carew of Carew Co.

ISBN 0985530502
ISBN-13 978-0985530501
BAT Series: Book 1

CCI Press - http://cobe.boisestate.edu/cci/cci-press/
BAT Series - http://cobe.boisestate.edu/cci/cci-press/bat-series/

All trademarks are the property of their respective companies.

Dedications

GK: To my wonderful, loving, wise, and creative wife Debby Queen, son Kyle Kaupins, daughter Amanda McGinnis, and exchange student Nato Peikrishvilli.

NKN: For aggressive learners everywhere, especially Tony, Chase and Quinn.

Acknowledgements

Thanks to many people who helped create (and finish) this project – Stephanie Chism, Bianca Jochimsen, and Joanna Lui for production magic, Paul Carew for design brilliance, and Boise State Public Radio, especially Erik Jones, for the wonderful experience with *Idaho Business Matters* for many years. We also thank Boise Inc. for its financial support.

TABLE OF CONTENTS

TABLE OF CONTENTS (expanded)

Foreword

Leadership is becoming more demanding and complex, so constant learning is an important part of any leader's routine. As the leader of an organization dedicated to continuous improvement, I also know that embracing creativity and innovation can help us improve performance. That's why Boise Inc. is proud to build a partnership with the Centre for Creativity and Innovation, which is part of Boise State University's College of Business and Economics.

The Centre offers organizations the chance to generate insight and "aha" moments in many different ways. One of the most recent, and one that we at Boise Inc. are especially excited about, is the upcoming publications from the Centre's new CCI Press. These publications will help leaders gain insights efficiently and in ways that are immediately applicable, which are important attributes in our fast-paced world.

Boise Inc. is pleased to support the CCI Press's inaugural offering, the *Business Aha! Tips* series. The *BAT* series starts with the book you are reading – on creativity. This book, like those that will follow, offers insight and knowledge in an easy to read, easy to apply format. Others will focus on ethics, hiring, global business, and performance.

I hope you take the ideas you learn from these books and use them to help your organization become a highly performing, highly creative one.

Alexander Toeldte
President and Chief Executive Officer
Boise Inc.

INTRODUCTION

On Bats

The logo of the *Business Aha! Tips* (BAT) books is a bat. We think the notion of bats works for several reasons:

1. **Good hearing.** Bats don't depend just on seeing, but rather on their ultrasonic hearing systems. They emit ultrasonic sounds that produce echoes. When they compare the sounds they emit to the returning echoes, bats create detailed images of any prey, even in complete darkness. In business, managers must sound out strategies to analyze what may and may not work. They also must actively listen to customers, employees, and other stakeholders to make those practices work.

2. **Wide ranging.** Bats move far and wide. In business, it is also important to move quickly to hit target markets.

3. **Symbolic.** Bats are symbols: Chinese link the bat with happiness and longevity, good characteristics to have in business as well. Bats are also associated with villains, like Dracula and heroes like Batman. Managers, like bats, may be villains one day and heroes the next.

4. **Adaptable.** Bats evolve. Over 52 million years ago, bats such as the Onclonycteris had claws on all five fingers. Now bats have claws on only two fingers of each hand. Companies likewise need to evolve to adapt to new political, economic, market and social conditions.

5. **Active.** Bats are active. We use the bat logo throughout the book to designate places in the book that ask you to act and apply the information you've just read.

6. **Cool.** Bats look cool. Enough said.

Why This Book on Creativity Now?

"Even if you are on the right track, you will get run over if you just sit there."

Will Rogers, American humorist (1879-1935)

Several years ago, Vietnam had a contest for teenagers to generate creative ideas on solving two big problems: providing clean water throughout the country and reducing air pollution in large cities. The prize: $2,500. That might not sound like a lot to some people in the U.S., so let's put it into perspective -- for what it says about Vietnam and creativity.

Vietnam is still a poor country. Its average wage per hour is the second lowest in the world, just above Bangladesh. The average per capita income in Vietnam at the time of the contest was about $1,200 per year per person. Granted, in the cities, it was higher at about $2,000 per year, but in the countryside, it was much lower, about $400. So any teenager who won the contest could probably more than double the size of her family's yearly income. The government's commitment to the contest reveals a growing emphasis on creativity in a country that many people would say is barely scraping by. Don't count it short. In fact, Vietnam may represent a trend that should disturb Americans.

A decade ago, evidence began cropping up suggesting that other countries were becoming more systematic about their need for creativity. Japan and China, the United Kingdom and Sweden, Australia and Mexico -- all showed a willingness to push notions of creativity and innovation more into schools, universities, companies and government. America has long led the world in innovation – in terms of research and development results, patents, publications, new products and services – but as the new century began, some worried about complacency in the U.S. For example, over the years, the National Science Foundation's annual report on *Science and Engineering Indicators,* described trends showing that America's percentage of scientific publications declined in comparison to other countries. China has now passed several western countries – the United Kingdom, Germany, and Japan – to rank as the world's second-largest producer of scientific articles. Finally, a recent IBM Global Services survey of CEOs from 60 countries around the world revealed that the number one characteristic they will look for in employees in the coming five years is creativity[1]. We fear the U.S. is slipping. So, now is the time to renew what has been such a strong part of America's skills, before it is too late.

This book is a step toward helping leaders and employees get excited about and doing things differently to boost their own and their organization's performance. That's what creativity is all about, pure and simple: doing something differently to get better. In this book, we'll the ways it happens, the culture in successful creative organizations and much more. We use a simple framework familiar to anyone who reads a newspaper or tells a story: who, what, when, where, why, and how. But, since this IS a book about creativity, we don't follow the list in just that order! However, our revised order should help you try to make sense of creativity.

- *Why* covers the reasons why creativity is important – not only in yourself, but in your organization, community and country. This "ultimate renewable resource" is truly remarkable and different from other resources: you can't claim it only for yourself, you can't hoard it, you can't pass it on, and you can't use it up. The power of creativity comes from generating and using it.
- *What* provides basic descriptions and dimensions of creativity and examines the myths we hold about it and how to misuse it.
- *Who* describes the types of people involved in the creative process. They may be entrepreneurs, leaders, team members, or even customers.
- *How* focuses on ways to use creativity – the processes and how organizations use them.
- *Where* covers the role of place and space as an influence on creativity – from offices to buildings to communities. Hint: creativity can happen anywhere, but some environments do encourage it more than others.
- *Examples* is a chapter that shows creativity in action – in many settings – from business to the arts, sports to communities. It's everywhere.
- *When* looks at trends – what's failed in the past, what's coming in the future.
- The *Conclusion* ties the ideas together.
- Since this is a book that tries to encourage aha moments, we include an *Aha! Moment Question* in

each section to help you cement and use the ideas right away.

- *Use it Now* is an end of chapter activity to jump-start your creative juices.

Many of the ideas come from original radio scripts written by Nancy Napier and Gundars Kaupins for a daily National Public Radio (NPR) affiliate radio program, called Idaho Business Matters, which aired on Boise State Public Radio from November 2004 through December 2011. The program featured a topic each week, divided into five, 90-second snippets per day. One idea every day – short and sweet. The radio format worked well for many listeners so we've adapted the short and sweet approach for the reader who has little time and wants a good idea. Each segment in this book explores one topic and has five short points within it. We have adapted the content for the book, making the ideas easy to grasp in small readable chunks, whether you read a single segment, a whole chapter, or the entire book at once.

Happy reading – and always look for creativity in unexpected places!

Use it Now!

"Use it Now" involves short activities that enhance chapter ideas. Here we go:

1. In your life, what has been your greatest creative achievement?

2. In your life, what has been a time that you have not done as well as you wanted to and creativity would have helped?

3. On a scale of 1 to 10, rate your level of creativity in your overall life:

   Low   1   2   3   4   5   6   7   8   9   10   High

4. Why did you rate yourself there?

2

What is Creativity?

In this chapter, we talk about fundamentals of creativity, from myths about it, to what encourages creativity, to how people misuse it.

Myths of Creativity

When you think about creativity, how do you go about it?

Some people might think they aren't creative at all. Others may say that only "some people" are able to be creative. What encourages innovation? Does time pressure help or hurt it? Does money motivate people to be creative?

Numerous myths surround creativity. And in fact, creativity is multi-facetted and each person can be creative in a different way. We all have some level of creativity and can develop our skills to enhance it, no matter what we start with.

So, what are the myths that many hold about creativity?

Myth #1: Creativity Only Comes From Creative Types

When managers talk about where they want creativity in their firms – they usually say R&D and advertising. They don't want it in accounting. But why not encourage creativity throughout organizations in areas where it makes sense to do something differently? Creativity is valuable in any part of an organization, often where you least expect it. Of course, you don't want accounting principles to be tossed, but the way you run the accounting department can perhaps be done differently, such as how to arrange offices or hours of work.

Harvard University professor Teresa Amabile has studied creativity for over 20 years. During the 1990's, she asked 238 people to keep daily journals of what they did at work. Then she analyzed the 12,000 journal entries and found some interesting things about creativity[2].

First, she found that managers think creativity should only be in *some* parts of organizations, but in fact, people in *all* areas have useful ideas, even areas that might not at first seem to be ripe – like finance or operations.

Another issue is how to encourage all employees to think creatively. Amabile claims that even though in the last five years, managers have talked more about creativity and innovation than ever before, it's still hard to tap it.

Aha! Moment Question: What creative activity happens in the "least creative" part of your company?

Myth #2: Money and Creativity

If you pay people more money, they'll be more creative, right? Money motivates people to do anything, right? It turns out that creativity might need a different type of encouragement.

Amabile found in her research, that despite what managers might think, money does not necessarily motivate people to be creative. In fact, she found that sometimes the promise of big bonuses or higher pay works *against* creativity. If people spend too much time thinking about whether they'll get the bonus, that might actually make them less willing to take risks (because they don't want to miss out on the bonus). Of course, risk is often what employees *should* do to be creative.

Amabile also found that employees in consumer products, high tech, and chemical firms want to feel they are fairly paid, but that *money* itself doesn't count as a huge motivator. They would rather have a real challenge and work in a place that supports and values creativity[3].

So, as motivation, consider the work environment, not just money! Providing employees with challenging projects and tasks could well be more important than assuming money will buy creative outputs.

Aha! Moment Question: If money is not effective, what other incentives might encourage creativity in your organization?

Myth #3: Creativity Under Time Pressure

When we think of the Manhattan Project, the race to the moon, or Crick and Watson's solving the DNA mystery, time pressure was always a factor. The Manhattan Project was a way to speed the end of WWII, the moon race was to beat the Russians and build scientific strength in the U.S., and Frances Crick and James Watson were competing against Linus Pauling, another scientist looking for the secrets of life. People achieved extraordinary tasks under pressure. So does that mean deadlines can help boost creativity?

Harvard's Teresa Amabile found that, contrary to what many people believe, putting time pressure on employees doesn't always spur them be more creative[4].

Even more interesting, she found a sort of "time pressure hangover." When people faced deadlines, they were sometimes more distracted by the time crunch and thus felt less likely to be creative. Even worse, distractions diverted their concentration, which is critical for being creative. So, managers need to shield employees – or employees need to find ways to "shield themselves" – from obligations that can suck creativity.

Aha! Moment Question: Has time pressure played a role – good or bad – in your ability to be creative?

Myth #4: Competition Fuels Creativity

Does competition within a firm fuel creativity? It makes sense that when people compete with each other or different units, it should spark creativity and innovation. In fact, that is not always the case.

Amabile's research on seven different companies considered competition among employees and found it didn't help fuel creativity. In fact, when people worried about getting credit for what they were doing, they stopped collaborating and working together to find solutions to problems. In that sense, competition actually limited creativity and communication within a group[5].

Rather, when people collaborate to share and argue about ideas, they often tend to be more creative. Sharing ideas is critical when people work on complex problems because typically no *one* person has all the best ideas. It's the old notion of 1+1 = more than 2. By sharing ideas, employees build on them, and make new and better ideas in the process.

So rather than ask employees to compete against each other, managers need to find ways to encourage collaborative creativity in work groups.

> **Aha! Moment Question:** Does working in groups encourage you to be more creative?

Myth #5: Downsizing and Streamlining

Money, time pressure and competition do not necessarily increase creativity. What about streamlining an organization -- meaning more tasks for fewer employees -- and in the process, encouraging employees to learn new areas and perhaps become more likely to see ways to do things differently?

Downsizing as a way to increase creativity doesn't make sense to Teresa Amabile. She studied a 6,000 person division in a global electronics firm while it cut 25% of its employees over a year and a half. Before the downsizing – as well as during it – creativity dropped dramatically. Amabile found that lack of stability and fear of the unknown hampers creative efforts. Even worse, Amabile found that creativity was down for several months after the downsizing ended. So when organizations reduce costs, they may discourage employees from finding innovative ways to get work done in teams better[6].

Aha! Moment Question: How is creativity encouraged in your organization?

Creativity Fundamentals

Innovation and creativity are certainly in the news – but creativity is a complex topic that can become overwhelming. So what are key things to remember? Let's talk about the fundamentals.

Fundamentals

Innovation is all the rage these days – but how do you boil it down to the fundamentals?

John Winsor, entrepreneur and author of *Spark*, identified three ideas that spur successful innovation.

First, he thinks innovation should be something every employee does, rather than just the CEO or a certain group. Second, Winsor and others think that creativity and innovation must go way beyond technology. This means finding new ways to interact with employees, customers, or the community. Finally, inspiration for new ideas is everywhere, not just in certain units or operations or even certain people[7].

So how can you start? Try a "what I hate" board -- since things that bother you can be great inspiration for ideas. Things like flip pops on cans that break before the can is open or kid-proof pill bottles when there are no kids in a house, or hole-punchers that clog up too often. Ideas will explode.

Aha! Moment Question: What do you "hate" that might spark ideas?

The Team

How do you spark innovation within a team? You might think, "It is already difficult enough to encourage individuals to be creative, but teams?" And this gets even more complicated if you have a very large team working on a project. How about 100 people working at the same table? Can they still be creative? Yes, with the right approach.

Former Nike executive Rob DeFlorio is an advertising whiz based in New York and London. His advertising agency, called Mother, uses a radical workspace design called "table philosophy." He puts 30 – or even 100 people -- in the same room, at the same huge table. Then, they just get to work.

Distracting? Yes, and that's what he wants. The benefit of table philosophy is immediate communication – it's much faster to have everyone around the same table – but it also fosters immediate interruption. The good news is that it means constant connection to the work, the people, and the ideas.

Table philosophy assumes that by having everyone at the same table, they will see the whole picture and not get into their small worlds and forget to talk to people elsewhere. Sparks fly as new ideas bounce around[8].

Aha! Moment Question: How can you use the table philosophy to make your next team meeting more creative?

Company Space

Creativity can ignite anywhere, anytime. Think of the most creative work encounters you've had – do they happen in board rooms? In your boss's office? How about on the stairwell? In the restroom?

Many firms have open informal spaces where employees gather to talk and generate ideas. Healthwise, a non-profit organization that provides information to help people make better health decisions, designed its building to be open – lots of glass and small meeting areas – so people see and meet each other very often. We might expect such openness and informality in the United States, but what about in Germany?

According to John Winsor, author of *Spark*, an engineering firm in Germany has a huge open area in the center of its building with a wide staircase that goes from the bottom to the top floor. The hope was that employees would use the stairs instead of an elevator and bump into each other, or "intersect," as the firm's managers would say. Not only do employees stand and talk, sometimes they sit, just like they might on the Spanish Steps in Rome. This gives them a great chance to chat with co-workers in an informal environment without having to set up meetings. It allows for spontaneous conversations and out of those intersections come some great new sparks for innovation[9].

Aha! Moment Question: Have you ever had a creative moment in an unexpected situation? Where and why?

Customers as Inspiration? Or Not?

Many organizations try to listen to customers for ideas on products or services to provide. Often, customer research opens up doors for new ideas that customers would like to see. But just how far should that listening really go? Do customers always know what they really want and need?

One software CEO says that he listens to customers "but not too much." Rather, his firm comes up with new products that customers don't even know they need or want. For him, customer input is valuable, but he doesn't rely solely on customers to tell him what to create. He figures those customers say the same things to him that they say to his competitors. So if all the companies react to customers, the same products will be out there. Then, how will his be different?

Instead, he uses customers' problems as inspiration for what they may need and not even know it[10]. Of course, there is a danger of being too far ahead of customers. Who was ready for interactive TV in the 1970's? Almost no one. But today, loads of people. That's the role of good leaders: balancing that inspiration without relying too much on customer input.

Aha! Moment Question: How much input do you think consumers should have on new product and service ideas?

Culture of Innovation

Maybe you wear Oakley glasses, those really cool sports goggles that whisper to you to be a little more risky as you swoosh down the ski hill? How does Oakley come up with the ideas for their designs?

For his book about sparking innovation, John Winsor interviewed Scott Bowers, Oakley's top marketing executive. Bowers says he and the other top managers try to develop products that have substance and purpose and...great design. The founder's mantra has been to "solve problems with invention and wrap those inventions in art." Think about those Oakley glasses again – they keep your eyes safe, a great invention. Yet they have real style. Sometimes they even seem like a piece of art[11].

To design and sell such products sometimes means the company has to take risks – to be brave – and offer something that may be way beyond what customers are ready for. Yet, in trying to be daring and fight mediocrity, Oakley has – so far at least – done a good job of blending purpose, substance and art.

> **Aha! Moment Question:** Could you create a culture of invention and art within your company?

Misuse of Creativity

Creativity is something many employers look for when hiring people. As good as it is to have many creative people in your organization, can creativity be misused? Let's talk about how some people might use creativity for sinister motives – like masking hidden agendas, delaying projects or even hiding incompetence in certain areas.

Ethics

Being creative in the workplace requires a certain degree of ethics. You might wonder how creativity could be unethical. Here's a scenario that could happen in any work environment:

Sally and Sue love to joke about Bill's comb over. "Who needs a weathervane? Just look at Bill's hair!!" They came up with loads of jokes about his hair. Bill hates the abuse. They rattled off one joke after another without thinking how their comments could hurt Bill. Creative, yes. Ethical, no.

Creativity without ethics is a misuse of creativity. Ethics should not be a constraint on creativity but rather an opportunity to create great new ideas. Sally and Sue could think of subtle ways to encourage Bill to change his hair without hurting his feelings. How about having a private meeting with him? Recommending hair transplants, toupees, medicine, the bald look, new hair color, or even doing nothing and accepting him for who he is?

Aha! Moment Question: Do you ever see similar situations in your workplace? How can you educate employees about using creativity ethically?

Hiding an Agenda

Have you ever pretended to be listening to an employee or co-worker? Have you ever had a hidden agenda while doing it? You are not alone.

Many years ago at General Electric, negotiations with the union broke down. The president offered to hear ideas from the union. He listened. Then he forcibly stated how his position was the only possible correct one. This negotiation tactic, known as Boulwarism, was named after the company president.

Creativity is sometimes used to mask a hidden agenda. A manager might solicit many ideas from employees to appear to be listening. After hearing their ideas, the manager might then still declare his or her idea to be the best.

A more subtle way to hide an agenda is for a manager to collect many employee ideas and then highlight ideas that support the manager's agenda and ignore those that don't.

Using creativity to fake listening and hide an agenda is a clear misuse of creativity.

Aha! Moment Question: How can you avoid hiding an agenda through fake listening?

Perfectionism

Creative people are full of ideas. But can they pick the best ones? And what can they do if none seem good enough? Perfectionism can be a negative influence.

Here's an example of perfectionism hurting creativity. Let's say Daniel has to write a report on how to create a new subdivision in the region. He comes up with many ways to arrange houses, schools, businesses, parks, and roads. Daniel considers environmental impacts, reactions from local governments, market considerations, economic forecasting and then…throws it all away. It's not good enough. Daniel is a very creative individual and wants the analysis to be right. So, he develops new housing arrangements. He considers other external influences on the subdivision. He will only settle for a perfect report.

Daniel misuses his creative mind by considering too many things and by wanting to create the perfect report. At some point, he has to say *enough* with the ideas. There is a deadline. A report has to go out.

Perfectionists need to realize they will never be perfect. So don't let perfection ruin creativity. Focus on deadlines and the task mission.

Aha! Moment Question: How can you turn perfectionism into a positive influence on your creative ideas?

Hiding Incompetence

Alas, some, people are not as competent as they pretend or ought to be. But often that's not apparent until they are facing a task they struggle to complete. Guess what they use to cover it up? Creativity!

For instance, Sam needs to design a new office space for his company, but feels incompetent at completing such a task. To mask his incompetence, he develops many office designs, hoping that the company will accept one of them. One way to hide incompetence is to develop many ideas -- hoping that one of them really *is* good. This shotgun approach can waste a client's time by having the client do much of the work.

Another way to hide incompetence is by developing many ideas to delay the inevitable failure. Sam could generate many terrible office designs and then ask to postpone delivery of the final report. That way, he can show that he's done a lot of work, even if results are not good.

Aha! Moment Question: How can you uncover people who use creativity to cover up incompetence?

Brainstorming and Follow Through

Being creative without following through is a waste of time and energy. Let's look at a scenario that many of us know too well: idea generation in group meetings.

Let's say you attend a meeting to develop a marketing plan. Different groups create, discuss and exchange ideas. At the end of the meeting, group members write their ideas on large sheets of paper and post them around the room.

Everyone admires the creative genius of the groups. Now what?

In general, posting lots of ideas on meeting room walls sounds like a great concept. The leader and participants feel good and can show that they worked hard. The room goes from drab walls to a plethora of words and magic marker colors. But actions speak louder than words and colors.

A recommendation to improve the follow-through process is to have the group organize those ideas and report on them -- which to pursue, which to dump -- by a certain date. The group can then analyze the ideas and act on them. Brainstorming without "brain doing" is brainless.

Aha! Moment Question: How can use you brainstorming effectively?

Use it Now!

Chapter 2 covered the basics about creativity. Now it's your turn to develop creative approaches to problems. Here's a quiz to start loosening your creative mind. List 12 different uses of a paper clip then turn the next page.

1. _____

2. _____

3. _____

4. _____

5. _____

6. _____

7. _____

8. _____

9. _____

10. _____

11. _____

12. _____

You could have solved the problem of listing 12 different uses of a paper clip in many ways.

1. Simply mention "12 different uses of a paper clip" on line one and be done.

2. Mention "Clip 12 different things" on line 1 and be done.

3. List 12 different uses of a paper clip—to clip papers, scratch your back, spear a target, etc.

In your list, you can think of a lot of different properties of a paper clip that can contribute to different uses. Here are some of the properties that could lead to different uses:

a. Can be metallic therefore magnetic—pick up iron

b. Can be plastic—children's toy

c. Can be bendable— button

d. Can be breakable (if plastic)—something to break for miniature karate practice

e. Can have two points that are sharp—pin for a bulletin board

f. Can have two points that are dull—massage tool

g. Can be shiny—solar reflector

h. Can be colorful—added to gift cards to make them more beautiful

i. Can be smooth—something to rub between the fingers as a stress reliever

j. Can be rough with ridges—inexpensive sandpaper

k. Can be small—rebent to be a coat hanger for a mouse

l. Can be large—significant art piece for a museum

m. Can be thin—part of electronic equipment

n. Can be thick—keep a door open

o. Can have narrow gaps—vise

p. Can have wide gaps—rebent into a ring

q. Can aid communication— wire between two soda cans

r. Can burn—materials to help cook food

s. Can melt—resolidification can help seal a hole

t. Can make a tune if struck—a new kind of instrument

u. Can vibrate—helps to play a guitar like a pick

v. Can bounce—can be the part of paper clip hockey

w. Can glide—added to a paper airplane to create more stability

x. Can be light—to tighten a helium balloon

y. Can be heavy—to hold a helium balloon down

z. Can be a topic of conversation—that is what we are doing now

Who is Involved with Creativity?

Organizations need different types of players when it comes to being successful at creativity. Below, we talk about critical roles that you need in your organization.

Creative Agents in Your Organization

Who are the creative agents or people who make creativity happen in organizations? Several are critical -- like creative entrepreneurs, creative leaders, and creative team members. Many exist, at lots of levels.

Creative Agents

When organizations want more creativity, much comes into play. One of the most important, of course, is the creative talent or people who come up with ideas and make them happen. But do different people do different tasks?

At least three groups are important inside organizations. They are the creative entrepreneurs, creative leaders, and creative team members. Creative entrepreneurs have the vision of what an organization can do – what's different, better, or innovative. Creative leaders are people who can take an idea and guide others to make it reality. Creative team members work at turning the idea into something customers want.

A last group is also important – customers who are willing to try new products or services or business models that come out of creative organizations.

Aha! Moment Question: Who are the creative agents in your organization?

Creative Entrepreneurs

Think of the entrepreneurs you know. They have incredible energy and take on risks. But many also have an uncanny ability to see things others do not.

Creative entrepreneurs have a knack for scanning their organization's environments and picking up on things others might not see.

When an artistic director from a theater in Idaho took a job in another theater in Ohio, he saw the possibility of an alliance between two geographically distant theaters. And it worked. Each theater now produce two plays and then ships it to the other theater – actors, sets, costumes -- the whole shebang. Four plays for the price of just over two. A few years later, he added yet another theater to the mix, in the far west U.S. and replicated the model. Now other regional theater directors are watching to see if this experiment works. All because he could see something others never had.

> **Aha! Moment Question**: Do you have a clear creative entrepreneur for your organization?

Creative Leaders

Creative entrepreneurs can come up with brilliant ideas for their organizations. But not all make sense. Often, a creative leader needs to step in to turn the feasible ones into reality.

Some people can be creative entrepreneurs and leaders. Nicholas Negroponte, MIT's Media Lab founder, does both. He came up with and now guides people in the development of an idea to bring affordable computers to villages in developing countries. His crank powered $100 laptop is tough and is low enough in price that schools in developing countries can buy it.

Some people are great creative entrepreneurs but need creative leaders for the next step. One CEO generates ideas that can lead his organization and the industry in new directions. But he's got so many ideas that another person – a creative leader – acts as a sieve to screen them for ones that are economically viable. His job is to choose feasible ideas and help guide a team to make them happen.

> **Aha! Moment Question:** Can you identify a creative leader and good "translator" of vision in your organization?

Creative Team Members

Your firm has a great idea that looks ready to go to market. You need a team to develop it and move it forward. What kind of people do you need?

A book called *Organizing Genius* [3] about great groups that have done extraordinary work – like building the atomic bomb or the fastest computer in the US – Bennis and Biederman talks about what makes great group team members. At least three things are important.

Team members need the confidence that they are going to be able to turn an idea into something real. They need curiosity to ask how to do something better and how to solve problems. Finally, a group needs diversity – difference in opinions and perspectives.

Some leaders say they "want diversity and they don't want diversity." What they mean is that they want the perspectives but also need people who fit the team and organization culture. It's a tension that is tough to balance but critical[12].

Aha! Moment Question: How can you build a creative team in your organization?

Idea Central: When Too Many Depend Upon Too Few

Albert Einstein is often quoted as saying, "imagination is more important than knowledge." In this knowledge economy, where ideas are the new currency, organizations need people who can help generate and spread new ideas. But sometimes they fall into a trap and depend on some person or persons to be the main idea generators. That's called Idea Central.

The Problem of Idea Central

Idea Central is where too many people depend upon too few to generate ideas.

Granted, organizations need creative entrepreneurs to find and encourage ideas. Yet relying too much or too long on such entrepreneurs can create different problems.

The founder and top manager of a highly successful organization has identified and found ways to exploit trends in his industry like few other people in the country. The CEO is in his early 60's and shows no signs of slowing down or wanting to.

Yet, his board of directors, managers, and employees – let alone industry colleagues – are irresponsible if they do not ask: "What if he weren't here? What would we do? If he weren't here to generate the ideas, would the organization survive?" It's a legitimate concern. Finding ways to avoid Idea Central, then, becomes critical.

Aha! Moment Question: Who are the idea generators in your organization and how much do you depend on them?

Long Twitchy Tails

When an organization depends on its top executive to generate ideas and direction for the future, sometimes it gets caught in a long tail that twitches too much.

When the top executive of a company comes up with the bulk of the firm's ideas, she becomes Idea Central. And sometimes the "tail" from an idea that comes out of Idea Central may simply be too long to be practical. This means it can take a long time for an idea to go from the top person to the area of an organization that implements an idea. In a fast paced market, that can mean missing an opportunity.

Also, if Idea Central's tail twitches – if she changes or revises an idea – the implementers can feel they are being asked to change direction and purpose. Such twitches may lead employees to become frustrated or complacent, neither of which helps get products developed and out the door.

> **Aha! Moment Question:** When did you see an idea that died from too many twitches?

Expanding the Periphery of Ideas

To avoid Idea Central, one organization tries to expand the periphery of knowledge within the company. In other words, the organization tries to get more people to understand the firm so they can participate more fully. The idea applies to creativity as well.

Expanding the periphery of ideas means getting more than a few people to take responsibility to find new ideas – for products, ways of operating, anything relating to how to improve or move forward.

Several years ago, in an interview in the *Wall Street Journal,* Target's three top executives described expanding the periphery of ideas this way: "You can't be unique in one category. You can't be really mundane in small electrics if you're trying to be innovative in textiles....you have to ... get more consistency across the board.[13]"

You also need consistency in finding ideas throughout an organization. That means everyone needs to be involved, and expected to find and generate good ideas.

> **Aha! Moment Question:** How does your organization expand the periphery of generating ideas?

Stealth Creativity

Some executives have to urge employees to generate and carry out good ideas. But some companies have cultures that not only allow, but encourage, employees to take on stealth creativity.

In the early 2000's, two Best Buy managers recognized the toll that the company's time-focused culture had begun taking. Employees in some units had to sign out at lunch, leave the name of the restaurant where they would be, and give their estimated return time. A bit over the top, thought some.

So the managers developed and implemented a new approach, without the knowledge of senior management. ROWE or "Results-Only Work Environment" focused on end results, not time spent in the office. It meant employees could come in the office at 9:00 am, leave at 3:00 pm, work at home or in the office, The "smashing the clock" practices were in place and successful for two years before the CEO knew about it. And once he did, he applauded the stealth creativity that the managers took on.

Aha! Moment Question: How would results-oriented management work in your organization?

How Permeable and Porous is Your Organization?

Geophysicists talk about how porous and permeable the earth is – or isn't. A porous substance has a lot of holes in it. Water or oil can sit in those holes, but stays in one place. And to find it, scientists need to drill right into the hole. Permeable matter has holes, but also has what are called "fractures," or small pipelines, between the holes. That allows water or oil to permeate the space more freely.

If you apply the metaphor to organizations, think of what's porous or permeable. Some organizations are porous – they have pockets or holes where there are lots of good ideas, creative people, and active innovations. But without permeability, those ideas may not spread around the organization. So to be sure good ideas spread, an organization needs pipelines or fractures or ways to connect the people and the ideas. This is another way to avoid the dangers of "Idea Central."

Aha! Moment Question: Is your organization porous – lots of pockets of ideas – and permeable – the ideas move around? Where are the pockets and why? How do the ideas flow (or not)?

Use it Now!

Chapter 3 covered the types of people involved with creativity. In this exercise, several questions discuss the most creative individuals.

1. List the most creative people you have met. What makes them creative?

2. Below is a list of some creative talent. Who are your favorites and what can you learn from them?

Mary Kay Ash, cosmetics entrepreneur

Fred Astaire, dancer, actor

Lucille Ball, actor

Yogi Berra, baseball player, manager

Sergey Brin, Google entrepreneur

George Washington Carver, inventor

Coco Chanel, Cosmetics entrepreneur

Sean Combs, Clothing, entertainment entrepreneur

Marie Curie, scientist

Leonardo DaVinci, artist, inventor

Phyllis Diller, comedian

Walt Disney, movie producer

Amelia Earhart, aviator
Albert Einstein, scientist
Debbi Fields, cookie entrepreneur
Robert Frost, poet
Bill Gates, Microsoft entrepreneur
Jane Goodall, scientist
Stephen Hawking, scientist
Bill Hewlett, Hewlett-Packard entrepreneur
Gene Kelly, actor, dancer
Martin Luther King, Jr., civil rights leader
Ray Kroc, McDonalds entrepreneur
Gary Larson, Far Side cartoonist
Estee Lauder, cosmetics entrepreneur
Mary Shelley, Frankenstein author
Frank Sinatra, singer, actor
Stephen Spielberg, movie director
Gloria Steinem, feminist leader, journalist
Barbra Streisand, singer, actor
Donald Trump, real estate entrepreneur

Thomas Edison, inventor
George Lucas, film director
Steven Jobs, Apple entrepreneur
Elton John, singer, songwriter
Madonna, singer
Steve Martin, comedian, actor
Paul Neuman, actor, entrepreneur
Lanny Page, Google entrepreneur
Rosa Parks, civil rights leader
J. K. Rowling, Harry Potter writer
Carl Sagan, astronomy scientist
William Shakespeare, English dramatist
Charles Schultz, Peanuts cartoonist
Sam Walton, Walmart entrepreneur
Vera Wang, fashion entrepreneur
Robin Williams, actor, comedian
Oprah Winfrey, actor, host

How Does Creativity Work?

Creativity happens in many ways, through many processes. It's not a mystery – or shouldn't be. In this chapter, we will talk about ways to spark and maintain creativity in any organization.

Aha! Moments

Have you ever experienced an aha! moment? All of a sudden, you understand something or solve a problem? It seems that most of us have them, but they often seem like unpredictable mysteries. So let's talk about just what they are?

There are at least two types of aha moments: the understanding aha and the creative aha. The understanding aha moment is when you suddenly "get it," understand something that you've been wrestling with – whether it's a foreign language, how to play squash or why your dog behaves the way she does. Boom, you see the reason, the rationale, or how something works.

The creative insight happens when you solve a vexing problem, when you come up with something new or different that you had not thought of (or perhaps others had not). It may feel sudden, but usually you've had to spend some time fretting over it. A variety of things occur on the way to reaching insight. So how then can you train yourself to make them happen more often?

Encouraging Aha! Moments

Most people say aha moments are unpredictable so you can't encourage them. Well, that's not quite true.

People use aha moments to solve problems and understand things better and there are many ways to encourage an aha moment. One way is by questioning basic assumptions.

Take a common assumption and turn it upside down. Say, a restaurant -- with no menus? What could you do with that? Offer food fresh from the garden, different every day. Have customers bring their *own* food and cook it on site. Or, the most obvious, offer a cafeteria.

At work, we always seem to set meetings for one hour. Why is that? Why not set them for 23 minutes? Or 41 minutes? Why not hold them standing up instead of sitting down? Why not have "walking meetings" – outside or in the gym on a treadmill? Aha!

One last example from overseas. In Hanoi, Vietnam, in May, it's "90-90:" 90° F and 90% humidity. Ouch!

So it's always surprising to see that women riding motorbikes in the heat are completely covered. On top of their sleeveless blouses, they wear long sleeved shirts that reach to their fingertips. Sometimes, they pull on opera length (to the elbow) gloves over the shirts. Underneath helmets, they wear hats that come down the napes of their necks. And of course, masks *and* sunglasses.

Why do they do that? Protection if they fall? Look at the curious behavior in another way – and challenge your assumptions. Covering up so much is sun protection. In Vietnam, a tan means you work on a farm. Pale skin means you are lucky enough to work in an office. Of course, when you tease them about their sun gear, they ask why American women *want* to be brown and tan?

> **Aha! Moment Question:** What is a problem you're working on? How would you turn it upside down?

The Value of Mulling

An aha! moment is an exciting experience, when you suddenly see something you missed or when you have a solution to a problem you have wrestled with. But you might ask yourself why you didn't see it before or why it didn't come when you were directly thinking about it?

When you are frustrated with a problem, sometimes it's best to step away from it. Funny how that works – you quit thinking about it and then BOOM – you find the solution. The invisible brain scores again!

You *may* think that you've stopped working on the problem, but your brain hasn't.

Those little neurons – and we have billions of them -- are making connections as fast as they can. But sometimes it takes a while before the right ones find each other. So even when you think you're *not* working on your problem, your brain is. Sort of your own personal computer and brilliant search engine.

Aha! Moment Question: When have you stopped working on a problem and then the solution "came to you" out of the blue? Think about the situation and see if you can recreate it to find the conditions that help encourage the aha!

Collective Aha! Moments

Can organizations generate "group aha's?" A classic WWII example shows that perhaps they could.

In 1943, in Shelby, Mississippi, two groups of Japanese American soldiers clashed like they were opposing forces. The group from Hawaii had much higher IQ's, better training, and looked down on those from the mainland. The mainland boys saw the Hawaiians as unsophisticated country bumpkins.

They fought so much that the Army considered disbanding the 442nd regiment, which went on to become the most decorated unit in WWII. But that came only after the group had a collective aha! moment.

One day the camp commander sent the Hawaiian group to visit two Japanese American internment camps. When they saw how the mainland soldiers and their families lived like prisoners in their own country, and then realized that those men *still* had volunteered for the army even as the government held their families, the Hawaiian group had a collective aha. Never again did the two groups scuffle. And, of course, became a hugely decorated unit during the war.

Aha! Moment Question: How could *your* organization experience a collective aha and learn something as a group?

Ripple and Upward Aha! Moments

Ripple aha! moments can happen when someone in one organization has an aha! moment, and then replicates the idea and the aha in other organizations. One woman in Hanoi, Vietnam, discovered just that possibility, in a completely unexpected way.

The woman works with children who have cancer. One year she put on a Western-style birthday party for the children who were in the hospital – cakes and candles, party favors and games, typical in the U.S., completely unheard of in Vietnam. But the kids and parents loved it. So several parents took the idea back to their home villages.

Suddenly, Western-style birthday parties were rippling all over Vietnam!

So aha! moments can spread, but can they be encouraged in those above us? In other words, can you encourage *upward* insight in organizations?

The deputy director of Vietnam's national Opera and Ballet Company has long tried to improve the orchestra and bring more traditional classical music into Vietnam. Rather than just playing Vietnamese music, he wants to bring the world's music to Vietnam.

He thinks that playing *only* Vietnamese music limits the type of audience that would come hear the orchestra. By expanding the range, more people might come to hear Bach, Beethoven or Wagner.

But a few years ago, the country's leaders didn't quite understand the director had in mind. Perhaps they feared that the Vietnamese music would disappear or that children would lose their Vietnamese identity if other types of music became popular. But the director persisted, thinking that a variety of music would appeal not only to Vietnamese but to foreigners who live in Vietnam and come from countries in Asia, the Americas or Europe.

So he tried to generate an "upward aha! moment" for the country's leaders. He made sure that now and then, at embassy and political functions, the orchestra played Vietnamese and some Western music. As the leaders began to see music as a way to build relationships with other countries, they began to "use" and showcase the orchestra and ballet when they interacted with their counterparts in formal events.

BOOM! The "upward aha" can now have even more impact.

> **Aha! Moment Question:** How can you help encourage "ripple" and "upward" aha! moments in your organization?

No More Aha! Moments

When several senior executives of very high performing and highly creative organizations said that, they no longer have big aha moments, that was surprising, and a little worrying. Would they continue to be creative and high performing if they didn't have insight and aha moments?

But after some investigation, it became clear that the senior leaders *did* indeed have insights and that they had made the aha! moment process a habit. Thus, they were constantly having small aha! moments because insight thinking was simply part of their normal way of thinking.

As they said, "of course we think differently, of course we look at problems from different perspectives, and of course we ask for different inputs." All of those techniques lead to new ideas, new solutions. And because the leaders use them every day and thus have small moments of insight constantly, the *huge* leaps of *aha!* are less frequent.

So think about that for a while – not only can you encourage aha! moments in yourself and others, you can make the process a habit, almost like brushing your teeth.

Aha! Moment Question: How do you create the habit of thinking differently so that you have constant small aha! moments?

Design Thinking

Does your organization ever face problems that are a tad....messy? Unstructured? Difficult to tackle? Have no fear. One creative approach can be quite handy in dealing with those pesky problems.

Design Thinking – New or Old?

What kinds of problems are you facing today? Ones with straightforward solutions – like where do I buy a new iPad? Or how to fix a broken toilet? You probably also have some that keep you awake at night – like what if the firm's CEO and visionary gets hit by a bus and there's no clear successor? Or how to deal with two managers who don't get along and it's affecting how their teams work together? Ah yes, those kinds of problems.

The messiest problems have no clear solutions and many leaders are looking for creative approaches for unstructured problems. One approach is a process that's gaining attention worldwide. It's called design thinking and was developed over 20 years ago.

The company that developed the concept, IDEO, has worked with a range of organizations, from hospitals to retail stores, high tech companies to bicycle manufacturers. In each case, the client has some kind of problem that its own smart people may not know how to tackle. In addition, sometimes the problem the client thinks it has may not be the real problem. So what might be some messy problems you face?

> **Aha! Moment Question:** How do you go about problem solving in your organization?

Key Steps in Design Thinking

Design thinking helps organizations come up with new products or solve solving messy problems. But it really requires a very different way of thinking than what most business or engineering experts use, starting with three key steps:

- Not jumping to a solution too early
- Observing the current or potential user
- Making prototypes fast to fail and learn faster

One of the main principles of design thinking is to resist jumping to solutions too soon. You may think you can hold back, but in fact, most of us are born problem solvers and we want clarity -- not fuzziness. Design thinking forces you to live with messiness and fuzziness for a long time. The reason: sometimes the problem you think you have may in fact not be the real problem.

For example, how many college campuses have signs about not taking short cuts across the grass because it damages the turf? Is the problem retraining students to stay on the sidewalk or is there another way to look at it? By reframing the problem to be one of how do we protect (some) grass and not fight human nature, some universities have instead put in walkways across the grass where people continually walk.

Aha! Moment Question: How do you identify the problem? Have you ever found you are trying to solve the *wrong* problem?

Youth Ranch Needs More Money

Youth Ranches around the country most likely all want to raise more money to help more kids. The Idaho Youth Ranch took its problem to a group of smart consultants who (eventually)

used design thinking to solve the problem. Here's what happened.

When the Youth Ranch managers asked, "How do we raise more money to help more kids," they also offered the consultants basic information, including a map of the state and location of the Ranch sites, the collection points where people dropped off items the Ranch could sell, the location of stores, and distribution routes. The consultants asked a lot of questions, like how the routes for collection worked, what proportion of items collected were salable and how many go to the dump. They learned that almost half of what people donate to the Ranch ended up in the dump and the Ranch then paid a lot to get rid of it -- over $100,000 in dump fees alone.

The consultants came up with loads of ideas, including a better inventory control system, rerouting trucks, focusing on new areas for collection of items that might be more possible to sell.

But when they calculated how much money that would save or generate for the Ranch, it was peanuts. So the consultants took a step back, used design thinking, and visited the stores to see what people buy.

Aha! Moment Question: What do you suppose they found?

And the Answer is....

The consultants eventually came up with a solution that makes $250,000 more per year for the Youth Ranch. How did they get there? Not by tweaking the inventory control system, not by sorting good from not so good items, and not by expanding collection to new locations. Then how?

They used design thinking – collecting facts and brainstorming *before* coming up with any options of solutions. Observing what goes on – by customers, by users, by suppliers – is a critical step in the process and one that often gets overlooked. In this case, the consultants visited the thrift shops where the Ranch sold items it had collected and watched what people bought. They found -- collectors. One man, for instance, buys only GI Joe dolls. He buys each for $1 and resells them on eBay for $10.

And that was the solution! The Youth Ranch now resells collector items on eBay. The result – a huge jump in money to help kids. But even after the consultants spotted a possible idea – internet sales – they followed another key principle of design thinking: fast prototyping. Trying ideas out quickly avoids a lot of time and money going into ones that don't work. So the group "tested" internet sales of different items on prototype websites to see which might be most effective. Once they found one that worked, the Youth Ranch implemented it and is now raising much more money than ever hoped for.

All because the consultants did not jump to the obvious solutions.

Aha! Moment Question: How might you stop yourself from jumping to solutions too fast?

Design Thinking Anywhere

The key principles of design thinking —such as not jumping to solutions, observing the potential or actual users where possible and trying out simple and quick prototypes— are usable in many settings. We have worked with organizations from an elderly care unit (wanted to better understand the experience of the patients and families), to a fish tagging firm (wanted to come up with new uses for its technology) to a university (wanted to find ways to make the student experience more meaningful).

When you look in your own organization at problems that are messy, think about how to frame the problem in different ways, how to understand what the experience of people involved may be, and how to test out one or five or 20 solutions as prototypes – and do it quickly and with few resources. Some firms create prototypes of web pages, of products, or of a customer experience.

For more information about design thinking, check out IDEO's website at www.ideo.com.

Aha! Moment Question: What might be messy problems in your organization that might be candidates for design thinking?

Hitting the Wall

You want to come up with a creative solution to a messy problem or find a new product idea. But the idea or solution just won't come. What can you do when you hit a wall? Let's take a look at ideas far outside of typical business approaches and consider lessons which come from…improvisational theater!

Pushing Through the Wall

At an improv show, you will see some wacky folks kicking ideas back and forth, coming up with a new routine or short scene that is funny or serious. The remarkable part, of course, is that they do it on the fly – or that's how it seems to us.

We talked with two partners in an improv company who have worked together for years. Even during a supposedly off-stage conversation, they carry on like they are still creating new skits and scenes. But they also admit that sometimes, things don't gel and they hit a wall.

In organizations, we usually think of hitting the wall or a problem as a bad thing, something to get rid of or solve fast. No so in comedy -- especially with improv actors. They see walls as opportunities to try new ideas. Actors use at least five ways to deal with an obstacle, and so do some businesspeople.

One is to just keep on pushing through it.

A marketing expert at an advertising firm often develops campaigns that hit snags. But when he hits a wall, he just keeps working – staying late at night, thinking about the problem all day, during meals. Rarely does he take a break until he has wrestled his way to a solution and luckily it always comes.

His motto: Just keep pushing and then, sometimes – AHA!

Aha! Moment Question: What if your boss gives you two hours to complete three tasks that you know will take five hours. How do you overcome this wall?

Tearing Down the Wall

Another improv comedy technique for dealing with obstacles is simply to tear down the wall.

In an organization, that could mean removing a person or group that obstructs progress. You know the type. This is the person who too often says, with great authority, "We tried that idea before and it won't work." Even if the organization tried something years before, even if different people are around now, the Great Authority knows how to put up a wall.

Another Great Authority might say, "You can't do that, it costs too much."

Or an obvious wall comes whenever someone you need says "What's in it for me? Why should I ever want to help?"

Without the wall, a team might just have a better chance of coming up with a solution. So what can you do? Try to find a way to remove the wall, to open up innovative thinking and perhaps generate new ideas for ways to get something done, even if someone else tried it before.

Aha! Moment Question: What types of walls have you torn down?

Going Around the Wall

You've tried just pushing through the wall; you've tried to remove any human or mental obstacle you might face as you work through a knotty problem. But you're still stuck. You feel like you've been trying to do the same thing over and over....and it just doesn't work. Einstein said the definition of insanity is just that -- doing the same thing over and over and expecting different results.

So what about just going around the wall? One theater teacher showed his high school students what he means by literally running into a wall over and over. He hits it, falls down. He moves sideways and runs into the wall, falls down. He tries the other side, no luck. Finally, he sees the edge of the wall and just walks around it. Success!

His point, useful for aspiring actors, is also useful for organizations as well. Tackling a problem the same *unsuccessful* way each time won't work. You need a new approach, some way to go around the wall, rather than continuing to run into it.

Aha! Moment Question: What walls can you walk around, rather than hitting head on?

Painting the Wall

Remember the old Wylie Coyote cartoons? The coyote backs the road runner up against a wall, figuring he has him …at last. The road runner turns, paints a door in the wall and runs through it. Wylie loses yet again.

Improv actors sometimes talk about getting out of a sticky situation by "painting the wall," or finding a way to turn an obstacle into an advantage. A remote location may be viewed as a disadvantage for a company that wants to become world class. So how can it paint the wall and turn remoteness into an advantage? One way might be to use the location as a "hide out" spot, to test new ideas and products before the rest of the world sees them.

Think of ways to use what seems like a wall, paint it and walk on through.

Aha! Moment Question: How could a little startup like Apple overcome the giant IBM in the computing business in the 1980's?

Ignoring the Wall

When you bump into a wall, what do you do? Tear it down, walk around it, use it? What about simply ignoring it and getting the job done?

When improv actors run into an obstacle they can't tear down, walk around or use, sometimes they just ignore it. A university team that wanted to design a program in a competitive market, going up against big name, big ticket, big reputation programs, hit a wall. The university had no reputation, no resources, and a potentially small market because of the remote location -- a lot of obstacles.

But instead of quitting, the team simply ignored many of the walls and focused on what it could control, built a dynamite program, and delivered it. By creating a new market, the program hit a sweet spot. The potential candidates chose to attend it instead of going to further away but bigger name institutions.

Maybe we should ignore *more* walls.

Aha! Moment Question: Pet Rocks were useless products that were put in a box and had no chance -- until they took off like crazy. What other products have had no hope, but had similar success?

Fantasies

Some people consider fantasies to be unrealistic and improbable mental images of something that may or may not be good -- like flying a kite to Jupiter. But they may also help spark creativity and stay competitive.

Turning Fantasies into Reality

Wouldn't it be great to be able to walk in a holodeck -- a computer-generated room -- and be able to pick up computer-generated objects just as they do in Star Trek movies? This fantasy may be far beyond our current technological capabilities, but the fantasy may have created computer innovation already.

Some innovators have developed a computer screen that you can literally walk through. The large screen consists of a thin, translucent gas that flows down from the top of the screen. The image might not be stable due to air currents but at least it is a start to the Star Trek world[14].

Fantasies do not have to be realistic to be useful for innovation. Even small steps toward fantasies – like a walk through a computer screen -- could lead to interesting and profitable innovations.

Aha! Moment Question: How can you turn a fantasy of yours into a reality?

Fear

One source of fantasies is fear -- of the unknown, of competitors, of business failure. How can fear help you develop new innovations?

You've just started a company that offers a new and exciting service. What if your new business has little or no competition? It could be easy to become complacent.

To enhance your motivation, you might consider a phantom competitor, which is an imaginary company that is more efficient and more vigilant about trends than yours might be. Your phantom competitor's productivity is so high that it could overtake your company unless you act.

Phantom competitors create an insecure state of mind that keeps managers from being complacent[15].

Such a phantom competitor might have helped Microsoft steer beyond its dominant software business and be more watchful of trends toward wireless computing and search engines.

A company can't be complacent when a phantom competitor is about to overwhelm the market. This fearful fantasy of phantoms may motivate managers to be innovative.

> **Aha! Moment Question:** What phantom competitor could you use today?

Fun

If you want to be innovative, think fantasy! One source of fantasies that might spark ideas comes from just having fun, with something like a hobby.

David was a sales manager with a Chevrolet dealership. He was doing well financially but was getting tired of his job. His hobby was woodworking. He fantasized about starting a business that let him pursue his hobby. This seemed unrealistic many years ago. However, as he learned more about woodworking, he discovered that his fantasy had real possibilities.

He retired from Chevrolet and started a new business that makes quality custom kitchen cabinets, doors, and other wood products. Thousands of dollars in equipment and staff later, he has become very successful. He is finally doing something that he really loves[16].

Sometimes fantasies can become realities if you have a strong desire to have fun in your career, carefully plan, and commit to achievement.

> **Aha! Moment Question:** What hobby do you have that could turn into a career?

Frustration

Another source of fantasies is frustration -- something like not getting your work noticed, when you *know* it is good.

Kris Kristofferson was an aspiring country music songwriter who dreamed of making it big in the music industry. He was frustrated in his attempts to get his songs noticed. So he rented a helicopter to visit Johnny Cash, the number one country music star at the time. Johnny accepted one of Kris's songs. "Sunday Morning Coming Down" became a hit for Johnny Cash and helped launch Kristofferson's career. Cash invited him to sing on the Johnny Cash television show. This led to a songwriting, singing, and acting career with songs like "Me and Bobby McGee" and movies such as "A Star is Born."

Fantasies that overcome frustration can lead to innovative solutions.

> **Aha! Moment Question**: Got any frustrations?

Learning

Ever fantasized about leaving the town where you live and moving to some place different – say, Hawaii? This fantasy is brought to you by the warm beaches of Waikiki, palm trees, and spectacular golf courses.

If you are considering moving or starting a business in Hawaii, you might first learn about whether that fantasy is doable. For example, you might read business and travel guides on the state. Yes, Hawaii has great weather, many international connections, and lots of recreation. But no place is perfect.

For instance, Hawaii is one of the most expensive places in the United States to start a business. The housing and land costs are very high, especially in Honolulu. Restrictions on land use contribute to the high costs. Transportation to and from the mainland can be very expensive. Numerous agricultural quarantines exist[17].

One of the things you can gain from fantasies is learning when to follow them and when not to.

Aha! Moment Question: Which of your fantasies could become real?

Use it Now!

We talked about design thinking in Chapter 4 where you can develop a product or service from the start. Below are some of the steps. Think about how you use this for a product or service that you are involved in.

Design Thinking

Understanding Phase:
Learn during this phase. Talk to experts. Conduct research about products and processes.

Observation Phase:
Watch how others interact with their physical spaces and places. They talk to customers, clients, and others. They ask questions and reflect on what they see. They emphasize with those who use products and services.

Definition Phase:
Become aware of people's needs and develop insights. How can we make changes that will impact people's experiences?

Idea Phase:
Brainstorm ideas like crazy to come up with solutions.

Prototype Phase:
Create various prototypes. It is better to fail early and often rather than stick with one model.

Testing Phase:
Test the various prototypes—see what works and what doesn't

Implementation Phase:
Make clearly defined tasks, determine the resources needed to develop the product or service, assign the tasks, execute, and deliver the product or service to the customer.

Review Phase:
Gather feedback from the consumer concerning your product or service. Determine if you met your goals. Discuss what could be improved based on clear metrics. Document everything.

Where Do Place and Space Enter Into Creativity?

Creativity can occur anywhere, but some environments are better than others in encouraging creativity. This chapter features some creativity-enhancing elements in different environments.

Innovation Beyond the Lab

Innovation can be everywhere – not just in the lab. Let's talk about how much innovation and imagination can happen far outside of a science lab – especially in organizations.

Apple and the iPad

Unless you have been asleep for the last several years, you've read articles about and maybe have the iPad. It's a computer-music-video-repository-library, so to speak. And it looks great too.

Apple's iconic products, from the iPod to the iPhone to the iPad, turned the digital consumer world upside down. If you read Apple's patent application for the touch screen, you'll see how remarkably clear it is, easy to understand -- just like the products.

Many Apple observers make the point, though, that Apple's success comes not from the technology side – although it's great – but from giving people what they don't even know they want or need[13]. And, best of all, even a non-techie can use them. As one CEO in software once said, "You don't make something simpler by explaining it *more*; you make it simpler by explaining it less." That's just what Apple does with its products. People don't care how they work, they just know they can use them without having to study a manual[18].

Aha! Moment Question: Could you make any of your products or services "simpler?"

Move Aside, Geeks

Often when we think of "innovation," we think of engineers and scientists. But not all great imagination comes out of a lab.

Innovation comes from many places. We may think of people working with scary equipment and lots of electronics, but often some great ideas come from unexpected places within traditional organizations.

Often the most innovative ideas come simply from understanding what customers want – Apple is a pro at this. Others come from taking existing ideas and figuring ways to get them to customers in a form they want.

In the late 1970's the Sinclair computer was really just a simple box and keyboard that hooked into the TV. The inventor – Sir Clive Sinclair -- was never able to capitalize on his brilliant idea so other companies, like IBM did[19].

So look for innovation everywhere – way beyond the lab.

Aha! Moment Question: Who is the most innovative non-technical person you know?

Creativity Under Pressure

When we think beyond a laboratory or engineering office as innovation sources, we should also think beyond just products, to services.

Trey McIntyre Project, a world-renowned dance group moved from San Francisco to a city near a ski slope. That year, the group set the date for a performance and then realized it had a problem. It was a long weekend and most of the city might head to the ski slopes. It also was Valentine weekend and people might have big plans. So, what did the dance group do?

They got creative. They repackaged the performance into a weekend adventure – a "Treycation" (named after the dance group's choreographer) where patrons could stay in the city, buy tickets and an experience. It includes dinner for two, a dance performance, a night at a hotel, and childcare. New ideas, new approach, new way to market. And not from a lab!

Aha! Moment Question: What other promotional ideas would you have for a group like a dance company?

Do You Need R&D to be Innovative?

Sometimes, the innovation we see is *not* something that people like as a consumer – but you've got to give companies kudos for looking for new ideas and trying them out.

We all understand that airlines are under huge economic pressure – charging for in flight snacks, checked baggage, upgrades. What's next? All those ideas are new, they fit the context we're living in and must create value for the firms, but gee, they are hard to swallow. And then, the simple hassle of getting through the airport makes it worse.

That's why you have to just smile at an innovation that comes out of hard times. Baggage pick-up and delivery services – sort of a FEDEX for your suitcases – have begun to take hold. Granted, they're expensive and not for most of us. But still, great idea, serves a need, and adds value (or deletes hassle) for some travelers.

Another way that innovation can come from outside of a lab.

Aha! Moment Question: Who do you consider to be the most innovative airline and why?

More Out of the Lab Examples

The laboratory is often a great place to find innovations, but a lot of innovations have come outside of the lab. Here is a list of a few more cool, non-lab innovations.

One company has developed a bicycle that can be transformed into a backpack. Ever heard of magnetic push pins that allow you to pin anything on a board without ruining it? What about a way to thwart purse-snatchers at restaurants -- thief-proof chairs that have slits for purse straps. In Japan, someone created a light and easy to carry cardboard portable seat[20].

These innovations might not be top sellers yet, but who knows. They might have potential.

Aha! Moment Question: What is one off the wall – non-tech – idea that might have a chance at selling?

Creativity and Community

Some people say the best way to predict the future is to create it. Many communities are trying to do just that.

The buzz about what makes cities creative has been growing like wildfire in the last few years. Many cities are trying to market themselves as good places to do business or live and often try to brand themselves as being innovative and attractive to creative people. So what does it mean to be a creative community?

Faces, Places and Spaces

As cities compete for economic development opportunities – for bringing new companies to town, for investment in new businesses or in education – many are looking for ways to cash in on creativity and innovation. What does that mean for a city?

In the last few years, the idea of creativity as a critical resource for nations, regions, and communities has become well known. Most of the research and actual examples cover three general themes – faces, places, and spaces. By faces, we mean the people and talent that a community needs to grow and develop in ways it wants to, rather than just letting it happen.

By places, we mean the elements that make a city a place where people want to be, a place that's easy to navigate, and a place that has some kind of "wow" factor.

By spaces, we mean the glue that holds the city together – the intangible culture or feeling that makes it a place people are proud of, connected to, and want to help improve. What are yours?

Aha! Moment Question: Who are the faces, where are the places, and what is the glue that holds your community together and helps it become more creative?

What's a Creative City Like?

When we talk of creative cities – we often think first about the place itself. So what are the characteristics of a creative community?

Three things stand out about cities that are appealing to creative people.

First is simply that people want to be on the street – they want to be in places that are bustling, where there are appealing restaurants and stores, and maybe even street artists. Think Seattle versus Phoenix. Think New Orleans versus Columbus. Seattle and New Orleans, unlike much of Phoenix or Columbus, have downtown spaces where people cluster, hang out and revive.

Second, creative cities often have something – a building, an open space, or some other icon -- that people recognize. They say "Oh yeah, that's the city with the great opera building, the French quarter, or the bridge with the shops on it." What does your city have?

Finally, creative cities innovatively use the natural assets they have. Northern Sweden in winter has little other than ice and snow – so why not build an Ice Hotel? Seattle's harbor and Minneapolis's lake are also assets that the cities have used to their advantage.

> **Aha! Moment Question:** Does *your* community have assets it's not tapping? What could you use to make it more creative and competitive?

Not Your Father's Library

When was the last time you went to a funeral or a wedding or a high school prom – in a library?

Go visit one of Seattle's and Salt Lake City's biggest tourist attractions – their libraries! Salt Lake's public library is the third most visited tourist site in the state of Utah, after the Mormon Tabernacle Temple and Zion National Park.

Designed by an internationally known architectural team, the library has become a Mecca for the community. You'll see 13-year olds, dressed in baggy pants, skateboards tucked under their arms, getting onto the elevator. Ask them what they're doing at the library and they may well say, "This is the coolest place to be after school. Look how you can see the insides of the elevators!"

The library hosts funerals, Halloween parties, and proms. There's even an outdoor amphitheater for small theater or musical production. As the librarians see it, once you get people *into* the library, they may even check out some videos or books!

> **Aha! Moment Question:** When you think of public spaces, how many of them in your community would attract the 13-year old skateboarder, the 30-something dad, *and* the retiree?

What Glue Holds a Creative City Together?

What's the "glue" or "space" of a city that holds it together and makes it into a place that people want to live in?

One type of glue that holds cities together and makes them work is collaboration.

In some cities, collaboration happens across sectors. People in government, the arts, business and education actually talk to and work with each other. Perhaps when cities have limited resources, groups and institutions can't afford to duplicate efforts, forcing collaboration. But maybe any way it happens is a good thing.

The Vietnamese have two ways to say "we." *Chung toi* means "we on this side of the table and you on yours." *Chung Ta* means "we together on all sides." For cities that have the *Chung Ta* (we together around the table) type of collaboration, it seems anything is possible. For all of the differences, "we" can find ways to work together. When people from business, education, the arts and government all work together, that's the type of collaboration that makes anything possible and builds stronger communities long term.

Aha! Moment Question: Do you have the *Chung toi* or *Chung ta* type of working relationship and why?

The Cocktail Party Test

You are with 200 friends at a cocktail party. You announce you are quitting your great job to start your own firm. What is the reaction?

If your friends become silent, look sideways at each other and go back to their conversations, he claims the city is not going to embrace innovative and risky ventures, the lifeblood of a creative city. If, however, people cheer and clap, the city is likely one that will thrive.

Aha! Moment Question: What would the reaction in your community be to The Cocktail Party Test question?

The Creative Campus

What is a creative campus? Steven Tepper from Vanderbilt University has studied the question and tried to make his own campus more creative. Some of his ideas might also apply for organizations, but let's start with university campuses.

Where Does Creativity Happen on a Campus?

Vanderbilt University's Curb Center provides experiences for students that encourage their creativity by bringing together art, enterprise and public policy in creative ways. The Center researchers needed to learn where creativity happens on a college campus, so they surveyed some 150 students to find out. Where do you think it happens? In the lab? In the studio?

Most said – *not* in the lab, *not* in the studio. Instead, students said they felt most creative and saw the same in other students when they were being creative in unexpected places -- like working on a homecoming float, standing in a hallway and having a conversation, or during a meeting of a student group.

The Curb Center found what many of us already know about creativity: it's not just in science or art. It's everywhere. But it happens most often when people from different disciplines or fields bump into each other. That's why it happens at a coffee shop or in a dorm or during intramural sports.

> **Aha! Moment Question:** If you think about *your* organization, where does creativity happen? In the hallways, in the coffee shop...just like on a campus!?

What is Creativity at a University?

When you think of a "creative campus," what comes to mind? Believe it or not, that's not as common across universities as you might think.

Many campuses are being more systematic in giving students tool kits to tackle messy problems in a variety of ways. We know that creative people come up with many possible solutions before settling on one, that they can make connections across ideas and disciplines, and that working with people from diverse backgrounds helps all of this happen.

Some universities are adding more courses in solving unstructured problems, or design thinking. Several put students from very different disciplines together so the biologists learn from the historians, who learn from the poets.

What would the equivalent be in a company? Put the R&D folks with the marketers and the financial whizzes sometime and find out!

> **Aha! Moment Question:** Do you have groups that might generate new ways of thinking, if they just talked to each other? How can you facilitate that?

An Imagination Lab

Boise State University has a new building for its College of Business and Economics. One large, open, industrial space is the Petersen-Hales Imagination Lab, named for football head coach Chris Petersen and entrepreneur Randy Hales.

The space is for workshops and classes, especially ones using design thinking, which we talked about in Chapter 4. It has funky furniture and tables that adjust to standing and sitting height. Lots of white boards and lots of toys to build prototypes.

The room is called the Imagination Lab – not the creativity or innovation lab – to remind users that imagination is necessary for everything we do – and to remember that we all have it. We just need to use it.

It also has five small team rooms where groups of students or managers can go for work and for inspiration. The names of those rooms should also help spark creativity and ideas. The Invisible Room has no windows, and should remind people to think about "what's missing" when they enter. The Imaginarium has windows on two sides, so it should shed "lots of light" on messy problems. The Aha! Room encourages the notion of having epiphanies, moments of sudden awareness and clarity. And the Reverse Thinking Room should inspire people to look at a problem in a way that is opposite from what they've done in the past.

By priming the pump, the space should help visitors think just a little bit differently than they did before entering the rooms!

Aha! Moment Question: How does space define how your organization members approach problems?

Creative Courses

When you spark more creativity on a college campus, what is the benefit? Who *really* gains? Only the students or others as well?

Vanderbilt University has started a program for a very few students who bring creative and an entrepreneurial spirit – and who eventually want to start and build organizations that blend both.

This new program delivers new experiences to students – from speakers to classes. However, the hope is that it will ripple to other students, to faculty members, and to administration.

Some of that happens on lots of campuses, in very different ways. On Boise State University's campus, we see creativity from many places – from the football program to an Imagination Lab. The lab is home for classes on ways to solve unstructured problems, necessary for students and for leaders in business and beyond.

Aha! Moment Question: Are there new ways to learn that you could use in your organization?

Creative Learning

The world of mobile learning is just beginning. Mobile phones, iPads, YouTube for universities, Skyping -- it's all going to be part of the ways that teachers and students approach learning. Some are using video games to transmit ideas and knowledge. Others offer courses where a student creates her own avatar that works in a company and solves problems. But learning is far more than equipment and software and many universities are trying innovations in all sorts of ways.

Many universities have used "live cases" for years – companies and non-profit organizations bring messy problems to classes and students wrestle with and come up with ideas for solutions.

One type of global live case class matches small U.S. firms with a class of international marketing students in Germany. The students look for markets in Europe for the firms and both firms and students get a cross-cultural, often challenging and always enlightening, experience.

A few are beginning to put students from vastly different disciplines on the same team – to design, build, and create a business plan for a new product. The students all come up with a product idea, then the art students design it, the engineers build it, and the business students prepare the plan to present to investors. And sometimes, investors put real money on the table!

Just as in companies, universities need to become more innovative in the classroom, and beyond. Tall task for places that still use techniques from Socrates' days!

Aha! Moment Question: How do you help employees in your organization "learn" in creative ways?

Use it Now!

Chapter 5 covered the location of where innovation occurs. Location can have a significant impact on the amount of creativity in a person. Communication, freedom to think, and individualism help increase creativity. But it can be found in a lot of different phases.

Match Game # 1

Match the invention with the country (answers two pages ahead):

Invention	Country
Car	United States
Helicopter	Italy
Soft Contact Lenses	Japan
Instant Coffee	Germany
Parachute	Netherlands
Barometer	France
Railway	Russia
Fire Hose	Czechoslovakia
Vacuum Cleaner	United Kingdom

Match Game # 2

Match the invention with the country (answers on the next page):

Invention	Country
Saxophone	South Africa
Ball Point Pen	Germany
Comic Strips	Switzerland
Cheese Slicer	Hungary
Skype	Norway
Clarinet	Australia
Instant Mashed Potatoes	Belgium
Heart Transplant	Sweden
Black Box Flight Recorder	Canada

Here are the Answers to the Previous Pages:

Match Game #1

Invention	Country
Car	Germany, 1886 by Carl Benz and Gottlieb Daimler
Helicopter	Russia, 1939 by Igor Sikorsky
Soft Contact Lenses	Czechoslovakia (now Czech Republic), 1961 by Otto Wichterle
Instant Coffee	Japan, 1901, by Satori Kato
Parachute	France, 1785 by Jean Pierre Blanchard
Barometer	Italy, 1643 by Evangelista Torricelli
Steam Locomotive	United Kingdom, 1804 by Richard Trevithick
Fire Hose	Netherlands, 1673 by Jan van der Heyden
Vacuum Cleaner	United States, 1869 by Ives McGaffey

Match Game #2

Invention	Country
Saxophone	Belgium, 1840's by Adolphe Sax
Ball Point Pen	Hungary, 1938 by Laszlo Biro
Comic Strips	Switzerland, 1820's by Rodolphe Toepffer
Cheese Slicer	Norway, 1925 by Thor Bjorklund
Skype	Sweden, 2003 by Niklas Zennstrom and Janus Friss
Clarinet	Germany, 1690 by Johann Christoph Denner
Instant Mashed Potatoes	Canada, 1962 by Edward Asselbergs
Heart Transplant	South Africa, 1967 by Chris Barnard
Black Box Flight Recorder	Australia, 1958 by David Warren

What are Some Examples of Creativity?

This chapter shows examples of creativity in business, the arts, sports, and communities. The wide variety of settings means that it can occur anytime, anyplace.

How Do the "Big Dogs" Innovate?

Creativity and innovation are hot topics for companies of all sizes. Have you ever wondered how the "big dogs" deal with it? In fact, maybe not that differently than your organization.

Online Democracy

Since its founding in 1995, eBay has been one of America's fastest growing companies. How does a giant online auction site implement changes in their business?

The easy answer is by using customer suggestions and opinions.

Online democracy is important for eBay. According to Thomas Malone[21], MIT professor and author of *The Future of Work,* eBay makes some of its most important decisions democratically. Electronic tools such as e-mail and online bulletin boards help eBay obtain information from buyers and sellers as input for decisions. Then, eBay changes its website only after it receives feedback from online discussions with customers. This online democracy has no official voting, but eBay managers use feedback to make marketing and web design decisions.

EBay started this policy years ago to ensure that buyers and sellers agree with certain changes to the website. Before this policy, eBay once changed the color of the stars showing seller ratings on the site. For two weeks, hundreds of messages flooded into eBay complaining about the new color and how incompetent eBay managers were to change it. Since then, eBay has used more "democracy" in its decision process.

Aha! Moment Question: How can you use more "democracy" in your place to encourage innovation?

Open Innovation

Large companies often have major R&D departments to generate and test new ideas, even some that may never see the light of day. But is that the only way to innovate? Certainly not. You might consider "open" innovation.

When a large company develops all products internally, it's "closed" innovation. Many great products have come from closed innovation -- like Hewlett Packard's inkjet printers or 3M's post-in notes. But these days, it's tough for one company to have all the best ideas from inside the firm.

An alternative is "open" innovation. Henry Chesbrough of the University of California at Berkeley, talks about "open" innovation as a method for large companies to gather ideas from much smaller firms in their industry. For instance, Proctor and Gamble has a goal of generating up to a third of its new product ideas from outside the firm. An example of an early success was the Crest "Spinbrush" which came from a startup firm[22].

By using "open" innovation, large companies gain leverage in brands and distribution systems by partnering with innovative small companies. This cooperation is often a win-win situation for both sides. The large companies save resources and give small companies a chance to sell and publish their innovations.

> **Aha! Moment Question:** How can your company benefit from "open" innovation?

Spin-Offs

Sometimes a large company's technology may not appeal to its main customers. But if the firm spins the technology off to a smaller company, it may still make money. In many cases, spin-offs from research and development departments can help firms develop new innovations.

Let's look at how large companies can develop new product innovation better by using spin-offs.

To improve its copiers, Xerox developed software ideas, but the firm couldn't find a market for them. So, Xerox partnered with entrepreneurs who did more research and then tested the ideas in the marketplace. The entrepreneurs who succeeded ended up doing very well and created their own firms. Perhaps you have heard of them: Adobe and 3Com.

When large companies license product ideas, they gain by linking up with innovative entrepreneurs who are not bound by big company customer preferences and who may be more willing to enter new markets. This means less risk for the large company and presents an opportunity for motivated entrepreneurs. These smaller companies may have different corporate philosophies and structures to adapt faster to customer needs and make the innovation successful.

Aha! Moment Question: Can your organization take advantage of spin-offs?

Everyday Hassles

Do you ever face hassles during the day? You are not alone. When people get stuck in traffic or can't find a cheap place to sleep in Tokyo, most just get frustrated. But some entrepreneurs turn their problem into an idea and make money.

For example, one entrepreneur who frequently traveled between Logan Airport and Boston was often stuck in tunnel traffic for more than fifteen minutes. When that happened, he lost his radio signal. His frustration gave him an idea to come up with a product to solve this problem. He created something called "tunnel radio," a radio station that covers all frequencies but is only accessible in a tunnel. The entrepreneur solved his own frustration – and made money on it.

Another example was a tired Japanese businessman who hated the high cost of hotels in Tokyo. All he needed was a place to wash up and sleep. In a moment of inspiration, he came up with tube hotels. Each hotel "room" is a tube that a customer crawls into. There's a window at the foot of the tube, a television, radio, and a phone. Each floor has communal bathrooms. Clean, cheap hotel room…all from a tired business traveler.

Innovations like these come from responding to everyday hassles in business or personal life. They often solve a problem that many others are facing in their everyday life and also make money.

Aha! Moment Question: What can you invent to solve your everyday hassles?

Poker or Chess

Should innovators be chess players—able to calculate the next fifteen moves just like a grandmaster chess player? Or should they be poker players—willing to take risks based on new information?

Let's discuss how large companies can think about technological innovation by comparing two popular games—chess and poker.

Harry Chesbrough suggests that chess is not as useful as a metaphor for technological innovation. In chess, one move can affect everything else that happens in the game. Grandmaster chess players can calculate their next fifteen moves just based on the opening strategy. Maybe that's why computers can now beat humans.

Real business life isn't like chess. Too many unpredictable events come up -- like competition, economic collapse, or sheer chance. And most of the time, these events or variables are difficult to predict before they happen.

That's why Chesbrough prefers poker as a metaphor for corporate innovators instead. Poker players make bets and lay down their cards based on limited information. The key to success is being willing to make changes, based upon incorporating new information -- or cards -- that appear during a game[23].

> **Aha! Moment Question:** How would you describe your innovative spirit? Are you a poker or a chess player?

High Tech – What Could Possibly Come Next?

How much fun would it be to lead an organization with a $3 billion budget and the mission to come up with cool innovative ideas? There is just such an organization, right here in the U.S.

What's DARPA?

What U.S. governmental agency has triggered more than one-third of all high tech innovations to come out of the U.S. in the last 60 years? NASA? National Science Foundation? Think again.

The U.S. Defense Advanced Research Projects Agency, or DARPA, started in 1958. Of course, those were the days when Sputnik and the Russians surprised the U.S. with its technological expertise.

According to an article in the *Financial Times*, DARPA head Tony Tether says he's got the best job anyone could hope for. If you think about the impact DARPA's had over 50 years, it *is* truly remarkable. From GPS to integrated circuits to the prototype of e-mail and Internet, DARPA's influence hits us all[24].

But Tether is more interested in what comes next. He sees exciting developments in green fuels, instant translation systems and vaccines that can be developed in three months, rather than years.

Aha! Moment Question: What exciting development do you see in technological advances this year?

How Does DARPA Get All Those Ideas?

Don't you love imagining where high tech can take us in the future? What about unmanned aircraft that could stay in space for years at a time with no input from humans? Or a truck that drives itself? There's a bit of the Jetsons in all of this but also some reality.

Only 25% of DARPA's work is for the Defense Department, but many of the ideas that have come out of DARPA can be used both in military and other applications. GPS is one.

DARPA director Tony Tether wants many more ideas and hopes that some will be extremely useful. He's using two main approaches to get there.

First, Tether is serious about increasing international collaboration. DARPA works with a company in the United Kingdom, for example, that is working on cameras without lenses.

Second, he asks for input from all of us. That's right. He's asking for anyone in the U.S. to give DARPA ideas. Using what he calls "public challenges," DARPA puts out a question or goal for anyone -- from scientists to amateurs -- to work on and send ideas. Even better, DARPA offers prizes for technical innovation in various areas, from transportation and medicine, to communication[25].

> **Aha! Moment Question:** Let's say you are part of the public challenge. What question would you send DARPA?

Finding the Next New Thing

If you heard there was prize money for coming up with the next best idea for unmanned trucks, would you jump on it? Apparently many already have.

The Defense Advanced Research Projects Agency is looking for good ideas. The director sets out what he calls "Grand Challenges" to encourage a range of people to get involved. The most recent was how to create driverless vehicles.

The robotic cars have to be able to complete a series of driving courses. The winning teams came from Carnegie Mellon, Stanford and Virginia Tech and split $3.5M.

Tether hopes challenges like these will spur young people to get interested in engineering and science. It's working and it's paying off for DARPA as well.

According to an article in the *Financial Times*, DARPA spent about $20M organizing the competitions and received about $100-200M worth of development work from the groups that participated[26].

> **Aha! Moment Question:** If you would set up a competition for a new technology, what would that competition be?

How Can DARPA Succeed?

What is the secret to success for a high powered government research agency that strives to come up with the next best high tech ideas? Could it be….people?!

Tony Tether says DARPA's employment agreements are key. The agency hires people on contract, for four to six years. Usually they come from universities and then return after the project closes down.

Because they are temporary, DARPA can protect them from the normal government red tape. The program managers have lots of power to make the projects work. Also, because the program managers are on staff for relatively short periods of time, the turnover brings fresh ideas on a regular basis.

Finally, because these managers don't see DARPA as their career organizations, they are willing to take lots of risks that people entrenched in a system might avoid[27].

Interesting way to organize and use employees. Maybe there are ideas for business firms working with universities as well.

Aha! Moment Question: If you were free to work with DARPA for three to four years, what project would you like to work on with them?

Pushing Patents to the World

We've talked about the ways that DARPA, a government agency, doesn't seem to act like a government agency! So what are the results of its innovative approaches? Lots of great output.

DARPA has come up with about 30% of the high tech innovations in the last 40 years in the United States. Many started as defense related projects but have spun to other sectors. The GPS system is one that many of us use. Part of the reason that DARPA has been successful at pushing its technologies into the general economy is its liberal patent policy. The university or company that develops the research, under contract from DARPA, owns the patent.

That means the university has an incentive to make the technology commercially successful[27].

The result -- some unexpected and yet great technologies.

Aha! Moment Question: DARPA is the master of spin-offs. Imagine something as simple as a light bulb. What kind of spinoffs could you have for that product?

Walt Disney's Magic

Walt Disney created magic. To the casual observer, it looked easy, with one brilliant idea flowing to another. But, like any good illusionist, Disney made something difficult look easy. How did he do it and what can we learn from him?

Disney's Childhood Creativity Sparks

Walt Disney's childhood gave him much grist for his future career. Disney's early childhood hometown, Marceline, Missouri, even today has the atmosphere of a gracious small Midwestern town. Farms, Victorian-style buildings, a broad street through the center of town...all of those images and the feelings they generated sparked Disney's appreciation for turn-of-the-last-century life that contributed to what became "Main Street" in Disneyland. His uncle Mike, an engineer on the Santa Fe Railroad, also sparked his imagination to include a steam engine driving into to his Disneyland Main Street Station.

Disney honed and developed his cartoon drawing skills early in life as well. He began studying at the Kansas City Art Institute at age fourteen. Working in the Institute's venerable buildings and grand grounds, he became part of a legacy of cartoonists that continues today.

Finally, Disney was fascinated by Abraham Lincoln as a child and later built a Hall of Presidents featuring Lincoln. Even as a child, he dressed up as Lincoln on the president's birthday and visited school classes, wearing a crepe paper beard with the mole and a stovepipe hat that he made by adding cardboard to a derby hat and then painting it black. In his beard, hat and his father's long coat, he wandered through his school, giving the Gettysburg Address[28].

Aha! Moment Question: What can you draw from your own childhood that might spark creativity in your work life today?

A Master of Experimenting

Like many trailblazers, Walt Disney worked at being creative. One of his secrets was to be a master at experimenting, trying out new ideas just as some gained success. For instance, after the success with the Mickey Mouse character in the film *Steamboat Willie*, Disney plowed the money he made into a new creation, a series of movies called *Silly Symphonies*. These films used different cartoon characters in various stunts and ploys while musical themes played out in the background. By using the symphonies as background music, Disney's animators could experiment with how the different cartoon characters could move or behave, a first in the film industry.

Experimentation like that also allowed cartoonists to try new ways of drawing the characters to make them synchronize even more closely with the music. The cartoon characters had a variety of facial expressions, gestures and movements. Beyond the drawing itself, the new movies also encouraged the use of new methods or technologies. For instance, cartoonists began drawing on glass screens, which would allow them to show scenery in the background, behind the glass on which the cartoon characters appeared. That meant that the scenery could be fixed, rather than redrawn for each print, allowing the character to appear to wander through it.

Disney's experimenting paid off. One of his early Silly Symphonies films, called "Flowers and Trees," became the world's first full color cartoon and won the first cartoon Academy Award in 1932. Disney dominated the category in the next decade[29].

Aha! Moment Question: Where and how do you encourage experimenting in your organization – with products, services or how things get done?

What Comes Next?

Disney never stopped experimenting or questioning assumptions about the field he helped create. One was the assumption about cartoons themselves. In the early 1930's, many people thought of cartoons as eight-minute segments. Why would anyone want to watch a longer program? Walt Disney set out to blast that assumption.

In 1937, after three years of work, Disney released the 83-minute long *Snow White* film to the theaters. It became the highest grossing film of all time and held that record until 1939 when *Gone With the Wind* came out. Yet, Disney kept putting out cartoon films that truly were long form films, from *Pinnochio* to *Fantasia*.

Disney didn't stop with cartoon films, of course. He entered the new world of television with a show called *Davey Crockett*. He started his own program and children's group called the Mickey Mouse Club. And, of course, in 1955, he opened Disneyland.

Interestingly, Disney not only built his own wide ranging empire with movies and theme parks, but his work inspired many others and many variations from his early ideas[30].

Disneyland led to an explosion of theme parks, from Disney World to the Epcot Center, from Animal Kingdom to the Hollywood Studios. The cartoon movies sparked completely live action films, like *Treasure Island* or *20,000 Leagues Under the Sea*, and eventually *Pirates of the Caribbean*.

All this after starting with nothing but cartoons!

Get the picture? Start with an idea that generates some success and then build variations, a classic part of brainstorming.

Aha! Moment Question: What spinoffs could you imagine from your current products or services (or from others in other fields) that would be variations that could succeed?

Learning from Mistakes

Despite – or perhaps because of – the success that Walt Disney and Disney Studios had over the years, they also acknowledged many mistakes. The good news is that Disney and others tried to learn from those mistakes.

One of the most prominent was opening Disneyland Paris. It copied much from the original Disneyland, from the design to the expectations for employees. But what happens in Disneyland sometimes needs to stay in

Disneyland (U.S.).   The cultural differences between the U.S. and France smacked the Disneyland executives right across the face. Europeans did *not* like having a complete stranger with a big smile approach them, say how great they are, and hand them a token. Their thoughts: "Why is the stranger acting that way? How can anyone smile like that without knowing me? Why would I take something I don't want from a stranger?"

The staff at Disneyland Paris had to change their ways.

They loosened the restrictions on dress and hairstyles. They added more French characters roaming the park, making a connection with visitors. In essence, the Disney staff had to adjust to the French culture to make Disneyland Paris succeed.

> **Aha! Moment Question:**   Mistakes happen. What are some that your organization has made…and learned from?

Imagineers

Walt Disney developed Imagineers who are individuals with imagination and engineering skills to develop creative ways to enhance whatever the Disney company wants to do.

At the Imagineering Campus in Glendale, California, the Imagineers represent over 140 different disciplines such as illustration, architecture, lighting design, show writing, graphic design, and computer software. Disney collapses the greatest variety of talent in a small area to produce new adventures for the public.

As a result of their collaborative efforts, they have created amazing things for their theme parks such as the Audio-Anamatronics Pirates of the Caribbean ride and the free-fall Tower of Terror ride[31].   For the cruise line, they created 765 foot water coaster ride called *Aquaduck*. There also is rotational dining in which guests move to three themed restaurants but are accompanied by the same serving team -- not exactly high tech but quite innovative[32].

> **Aha! Moment Question:** If you had ten experts from different fields helping you create, what would they work on?

Innovation in Idaho

Innovation is a buzzword that many people associate with organizations or specific products. What about cities or even states? Can they be innovative? Of course they can. Because we are based in Boise, Idaho, we'll look at the level of innovation here, as an example of what could be anywhere in the U.S.

When people think of Idaho, many think of potatoes. But guess what? Like any other place with an icon, Idaho is a lot more than potatoes. From computer hardware to agricultural products, from energy technology to software, Idaho has it covered. For years, the state has had the highest patents per capita of any state, thanks in large part to Hewlett-Packard and Micron. So what can a state – like Idaho and beyond – do to encourage innovation?

Examples of Idaho Innovations

You might ask, "What in the world do companies in Idaho create that's innovative?" With 974 patents awarded in 2010, Idaho topped the nation with per capita patents. Computer hardware and semiconductor manufacturing are two of the biggest computer technology sectors in Idaho. In fact, almost 80% of the patents awarded in 2010 went to the top three technology/computer organizations in the state. These patents include innovations such as computer chips used in high-performance satellite transmission or energy-efficient memory products designed to reduce data center server power consumption[33].

Idaho is also home to other innovations that might surprise you. For example, Microbial-Vac Systems developed a hand-held vacuum that allows food inspectors and public safety officials to efficiently collect germs from virtually any wet or dry surface. After they collect the germs, scientists can study them in a lab. Or the Rodenator, which helps farmers eliminate gophers and other underground pests by collapsing their tunnels.

Innovation in Idaho is much more than growing potatoes and that probably holds for your state too.

Aha! Moment Question: How creative is your state?

Venture Forum

Innovation does not happen out of the blue. Companies need to be encouraged to continuously come up with cutting edge products. How can states support innovation? Large firms often have funding for innovation. But sometimes, companies with the best business ideas need extra money to go to the next level. So what can they do?

In Idaho, the Annual Intermountain Venture Forum (IVF) is an opportunity for companies in the Mountain West Region to connect with investors looking for great ideas. The Forum celebrates entrepreneurs who have the ideas and drive to build a strong economic base for the state. Often, serial entrepreneurs are the "catalysts" that attract venture capital funding to the area. Annually, the Forum features a dozen of the Intermountain West's most promising companies.

Venture capital firms look for investment opportunities in companies that have the potential to be $100M companies, can generate long-term profits, and have leaders who are passionate and ready to run fast.

Aha! Moment Question: How can you support innovation in your state?

Innovation Awards

Innovation takes nurturing, in many ways. One way is to encourage competition, which pushes firms to innovate to stay ahead of the pack. To foster a competitive and innovative spirit, a regional business law firm, Stoel Rives, launched the Idaho Innovation Awards. The program recognizes innovations and the Idaho companies behind them. Every year, program organizers honor sixteen innovations at an Awards Luncheon. Also involved in the program are the state's Department of Commerce Office of Science and Technology, Hewlett-Packard and the *Idaho Business Review.*

The awards recognize product and service innovations in a wide range of fields. The winners come from biosciences, computer hardware and software and energy. The qualifying innovations were recently developed by an Idaho-based company or by Idaho residents.

The program usually receives more than 50 nominations every year. The candidates complete nomination forms describing the innovation, and how it is useful and innovative. A selection committee made of leaders from the high-tech industry, business and education communities evaluates the entries.

Aha! Moment Question: What programs encourage innovation in your state?

Students, Create!

Boise, Idaho, is often highly ranked as a place to start a business and a place where innovation happens. But it doesn't happen without a lot of encouragement, starting with what goes on in universities. But how do you teach students to be innovative and make them think creatively? Many schools offer courses, budding entrepreneur courses, that help them learn to write business plans and test out those plans. But few help them find business ideas.

At Boise State, professors from engineering and business have taught courses on creativity and innovation. Student backgrounds range from engineering and business, to pre-med, English and education. In the course, they increased their creative skills, learned how to innovate, and prototyped a product or service.

This course is especially useful for engineers. They tend to be great at designing and building products – but not so strong in the creation of new ideas for products or in understanding how to take them to market. By collaborating with students from other disciplines, all must look at concepts and ideas in new ways.

Aha! Moment Question: How can you teach others how to be more creative?

Creativity Index

Imagine if there were an index that could measure the level of creativity and innovation in a city or region or state? Just think how useful that might be to identify what enhances or inhibits innovation and what could be done about it!

Boise State students worked together with students in Heidelberg, Germany, to create an index to help measure the levels of creativity and innovation in their respective cities. The goal was to identify the factors that influence organizational creativity and innovation – in good or bad ways. They looked at factors like government policy, access to cultural events, or at similar types of creative organizations.

Years ago, University of Toronto professor Richard Florida generated a very simple and widely publicized index[34]. He used three measures that ranked cities on their openness to creativity. The measures were technology or patents per capita, talent or the number and types of people and professions in a city, and tolerance or openness to diverse people and ideas. What other criteria might be important and how might cities use them?

Aha! Moment Question: How do you measure creativity in your city?

Use it Now!

Chapter 6 focused on lots of examples of how corporations came up with ideas for new innovations. It's your turn to come up with innovations by creating spinoff products. This exercise will help you get started.

Spinoff Product Exercises

The following exercises test your brainstorming ability. In brainstorming, remember to follow the following four rules:

1. Focus on quantity over quality.
2. Even crazy ideas are acceptable---really.
3. Don't criticize anything you put down.
4. Build on ideas that you have. If you think about building a bird house, why not also build a bird condo, bird apartment, bird park, bird city, bird planet, bird solar system or bird galaxy.

In the spinoff exercises on the next pages, you will enter various words off the top of your head. Develop alternate new words at each level. Don't overthink or spend too much time thinking of the next item on the list. You can even backtrack and repeat old gems -- this is a brainstorm so go for it. See what interesting new spinoff products you come up with. You might end up with some interesting products at the bottom of your list. You might even have some interesting products in the middle of your list.

In this first set of spinoffs, begin with a location of a product and the product itself. Spinoff 1 is inspired by something found in the news: Tunnel Radio really does exist in Boston. This is a radio station that kicks in when you enter a long tunnel[35]. Spinoff 2 also was found in the news.

Spinoff 1

Location	Product
1. Tunnel	1. Radio
1. Tunnel	2. Television
3. Rooftop	2. Television
3. Rooftop	4. Microwave
5. _____	4. Microwave
5. _____	6. _____
7. _____	6. _____

Spinoff 2

Location	Product
1. Business	1. Plan
1. Business	2. Plane
3. Oregon	2. Plane
3. Oregon	4. Crackers
5. Seaside	4. Crackers
5. Seaside	6. _____
7. _____	6. _____

7. _____

8. _____

9. _____

8. _____

9. _____

10. _____

10. _____

11. _____

11. _____

12. _____

7. _____

8. _____

9. _____

8. _____

9. _____

10. _____

10. _____

11. _____

11. _____

12. _____

The next spinoffs link two seemingly unrelated objects. A capsule hotel is a popular hotel in Japan in which a large number of extremely small rooms are grouped together for people who do not need much overnight accommodations[36]. String cheese is just an innovation coming from personal experience.

Spinoff 3

Object	Object
1. Capsule	1. Hotels
2. Paper	1. Hotels
2. Paper	3. Calculator
4. Couch	3. Calculator
4. Couch	5. _____
6. _____	5. _____
6. _____	7. _____

Spinoff 4

Object	Object	Object
1. String	1. Cheese	
1. String	2. Door	
3. Barnacle	2. Door	
3. Barnacle	4. Knife Handle	
5. Golf Tee	4. Knife Handle	
5. Golf Tee	6. _____	
7. _____	6. _____	

7. _____

8. _____

9. _____

8. _____

9. _____

9. _____

10. _____

10. _____

11. _____

9. _____

10. _____

11. _____

The next spinoffs link an adjective to an object. Spinoff 5 was inspired by personal experiences of walking into a realtor's open house. The house had many modern features including a countertop that glowed with lights in it. The same house had door-handles that appeared to be like jewelry as shown with Spinoff 6. Sometimes personal experiences can lead to great new product ideas.

Spinoff 5

Adjective	Object
1. Sunny	1. Countertops
1. Sunny	2. Cell Phones
3. Soft	2. Cell Phones
3. Soft	4. _____
5. _____	4. _____
5. _____	6. _____
7. _____	6. _____

Spinoff 6

Adjective	Object
1. Sparkling	1. Door Handles
2. Soft	1. Door Handles
2. Soft	3. Pens
4. Invisible	3. Pens
4. Invisible	5. _____
6. _____	5. _____
6. _____	7. _____

7. _____ 8. _____

9. _____ 8. _____

9. _____ 10. _____

11. _____ 10. _____

11. _____ 12. _____

8. _____ 7. _____

8. _____ 9. _____

10. _____ 9. _____

10. _____ 11. _____

12. _____ 11. _____

When Will Creativity End?

When will creativity end? We hope never. In this chapter, we look at two remarkably different times that will show it will never end. The defunct past with out-of-date products may seem hopeless but is still an opportunity for creativity. The future is boundless with great ideas.

Defunct Products

Is there any use for something that is out of date? S&H Green Stamps, rotary dial phones, and printed encyclopedias are among the many defunct products. So what might we learn from them?

Rotary Dial Phones

Remember rotary dial phones? They gave way to punch button phones, and then cell phones, Skype, and many other communication devices. They have helped define what is defunct.

According to Jessica Handler[37] who looked at what happened to rotary dial phones in defunctmagazine.com, such phones were black, heavy, square, and sat on tables like obedient pets. They had a standard shape and sound. They were always tethered to a wall.

Rotary phones are defunct because they are out of date, out of mind, and out of use. They represent years of stagnation in product development. Museums would be eager to snatch them up. More creative and practical products such as cell phones, iPads, Skype, and apps dominate the scene. But, there are increasingly nostalgic apps that simulate the slowness and sound of rotary phones on cell phones.

Aha! Moment Question: How are your products and services? Do they have that defunct feel? Are they stagnant? How much are you working on new ideas?

Encyclopedias

Now that the Internet has taken over, is there any place for a hard copy encyclopedia -- or for that matter, a hard copy book?

Hard copy encyclopedias have faced difficult times with the convenience of the Internet. So some publishers have become more creative in their pursuit for the consumer dollars.

Wikipedia has embraced the Internet with consumer contributions for free but with plenty of ads to make money. The historical encyclopedias have tried to capture Internet interest by using great visuals, in-depth articles, and expert authors.

Encyclopedic books have provided large visual displays that show relationships between places, people, and events that would be difficult to show on a small computer screen. That's why the print encyclopedias may still have a chance, at least in new ways.

Aha! Moment Question: What would be an example of an encyclopedic book that would be useful for yourself? Example: a detailed book on gardening.

Edsel

The 1950's automobile called the Edsel was defunct when it came out. Its design was bad and construction was poor.

Although the Edsel was a disaster from the start, today there is a bit of nostalgia for the car. It is something of a museum piece that a collector would cherish not only for its history, but also for its unique design with its classic 1950's look.

Yes, the Edsel is defunct. But with a slight remarketing as a nostalgic vehicle, a product like the Edsel can take off in the car show marketplace.

Rotary dial phones and phonographs can also be remarketed this way in order to capture the nostalgic side of individuals.

Defunct is only defunct if it is perceived to be defunct. It is in the eye of the beholder. If the perception changes, a defunct product can become an instant hit.

Aha! Moment Question: What impractical object in your house can be retooled to be made practical in a totally different way?

Baseball

Major league baseball has been around for over a hundred years. Its rules have not changed much and other sports, such as football, have become more popular.

Wait a minute. Baseball is not defunct. Yes, the game has only seven minutes of action in every nine innings. Yes, the game is not timed like football and basketball. Yes, it's harder to see the ball on TV or the Internet than a football or basketball. But there are other ways of making the game pretty cool.

In major league parks today, huge scoreboards show the replays, provide detailed stats, cheer up the crowd, and give sound effects. A wide variety of promotions occur between innings.

The Internet features up-to-the-second scores with apps and social networks for each team.

Commentators analyze those seven minutes of action with top ten highlights, worst plays, best homers, and every other combination you can imagine.

Relevance to the fans, yes. Defunct, no.

Aha! Moment Question: Could you make chess and curling more exciting?

S&H Green Stamps

Back in the 1960's, S&H Green stamps were a classic way grocery stores motivated customers to shop more. You bought products from the grocery stores and got green stamps. You licked those stamps and put them into a book.

Once you filled the books, you traveled to an S&H Redemption Center to claim fabulous products, depending on how many books with green stamps you filled.

But, S&H Green Stamps were a pain. Filling those books with stamps was hard. Redemption Center checkers took their time checking that each page was full of stamps.

Nowadays, similar promotions come on one page in which the lucky winner needs only one or two stamps. Sometimes sending your winnings electronically will work.

S&H didn't adapt with the times. They may have had a great product for the 1960's when there was more free time at home. But for today's busier schedules, faster grocery promotions are the ticket.

Aha! Moment Question: What are at least three ways grocery stores are trying to sell more products to you?

Innovation Trends

How does innovation happen? In today's global and interconnected world, it is getting easier to track innovation. Especially with the Internet, we have no excuse not to know about innovations going on worldwide. So let's discuss trends in innovation that come from outside the U.S., ranging from ones that tackle information overload to ways to make our lives easier.

"Info Lust" and Information Overload

Do you Google daily? Do you search for the cheapest airfare or hotel? Do you find eBay or other online shopping sites addictive? Forget information overload! It seems that many of us have "Info Lust!"

Apparently many of us want more information on a daily basis than ever before. And with more sites popping up every day, we can enjoy "Info Lust" without noticing the information overload that comes with it.

The website Trendwatching.com tracks changes and trends worldwide. One newsletter claims that instead of feeling information overload, many of us want more information and that some consumers are "lusting" for information about the best or cheapest or first of any number of products and services.

Apparently, a human need is driving this lust for more information – the need for power, knowledge and information. Transparency and availability of information online helps spur this lust and business firms are ready and willing to meet the demand by continuously providing more information on the web.

Aha! Moment Question: Have you got "Info Lust?" How do you get your fix and what sites do you troll?

Massclusivity

What are some of the trends that affect innovation around the world? One website tracks trends so it's easy to know.

Trendwatching.com has reported on a trend called "massclusivity," which is luxury for the masses. The more customers have access to products and services, the more they want exclusivity because now "everyone" can have certain mass consumer items. Thus, the trend means we will mean more upgrading of products and services. Since individual and family income is increasing in many parts of the world, especially the developing world, "massclusivity" may increase.

It's happening from grocery stores to transportation. MPreis, an Austrian supermarket chain, calls itself the Seriously Sexy Supermarket. The stores are set in the Tyrolean Alps and each has dramatic architecture. The setting provides a great experience for consumers and its prices aren't higher than competitors so the draw is clear.

Transportation is also hit by "massclusivity." Escape Rentals, a New Zealand camper rental company, has commissioned artists to turn their rental vans into art on wheels. And the Japanese airliner StarFlyer has sleek black and white planes, all leather seats, LCD monitors for inflight TV, and laptop power ports. All of these companies found ways to use "massclusivity" – or bringing luxury to the masses.

Aha! Moment Question: Can you use the idea of "massclusivity" in your organization?

Making Harried Lives Easier

When someone invents a product or a service that makes our lives easier, don't we cheer? On the other hand, it might be something that you never thought you needed until you actually have it or have access to it. Trendwatching.com offers an easy way to follow innovations worldwide that are supposed to make our harried lives easier.

Not all meetings can take place in a Starbucks. Sometimes business people need a more professional setting but may not have a formal office. The answer: business community centers. Throughout Canada, Coffee Office offers meeting space, workstations, Internet access and a café, all in a professional setting. Small business owners, or traveling managers, pay a monthly fee. They then have access to the facilities in numerous Coffee Offices around the country.

And what can you do when you forget to charge your mobile phone? Visit Charge Box. In the United Kingdom, a company called Charge Box has lockers in over 1,000 locations around the country in train stations, stadiums, and office buildings. Each locker has three different chargers – for your phone, your computer, or your iPod. You pay with cash or by sending an SMS message to a code. The locker opens and the charging begins.

Aha! Moment Question: Which innovations have recently changed your life?

Niche Networks

In recent years, many of us have gotten into an online routine and it can be difficult to break it. We check certain sites every day and may get distracted discovering new sites. And lots of those websites want to take advantage of our addiction.

Trendwatching.com reports on the types of services springing up to exploit our online habit. They are called "niche networks." People of all ages have jumped on sites like Facebook and LinkedIn that allow members to connect.

Other networks focus on specific interests. For example, Meshtennis.com is a social network for tennis players – to find other players in their areas. No doubt other sports and hobby networks are springing up on the web to compete for our attention.

Aha! Moment Question: How do "niche networks" influence your life? What can you do to avoid them taking over your life?

Forever Trends

Some trends come and go. But others stay and can offer opportunities for ambitious entrepreneurs. Some longer lasting trends include alternative energy source ideas, driving services for aging baby boomers, and healthy fast food for kids.

Recycling only goes so far. Consumers also want to explore other ways to be sustainable and to also save energy. Solar and wind energy has been a very hot topic for a while. For example, Windsave, a British/Scottish venture, makes small, quiet windmills for homes. Each windmill generates about 1kw of electricity, enough to run a DVD player, computer and fridge.

Second, as baby boomers worldwide age, driving services are popping up. For example, Driving Miss Daisy is a Canadian cab and companion service for seniors. They take seniors to appointments or shopping, all with extra security and at affordable prices.

Finally, parents often try to instill good health habits – and food – in their kids. A Dutch firm called Lunch4Kids lets parents order lunches online for their school children, including a sandwich, drink, fruit and snack. The lunches are delivered to participating schools each morning.

Aha! Moment Question: What are some interesting trends that you have discovered recently?

Use it Now!

Chapter 7 looks to the past and the future in terms of creativity. In this exercise, we focus on the future.

Product Development: Take one product and divide it up into five major categories that you will manipulate. Continue to make wild alterations to the parts until you come up with satisfactory alternatives and lock them in. An example follows: Change one to four things at a time until you lock on to something you like concerning a picture frame.

Product #1: Picture Frame

Part 1 Frame	Part 2 Marketing	Part 3 Base	Part 4 Picture	Part 5 Size
Rectangle Brown	Retail Walmart	Picture Stand	Standard Photo	8 by 11

Rectangle Brown	Internet	Picture Stand	Movies/photos downloaded from a flash drive	8 by 11
_____	_____	_____	_____	_____
_____	_____	_____	_____	_____
_____	_____	_____	_____	_____
_____	_____	_____	_____	_____

Now it is your turn to name your own product and think of five dimensions of that product on your own.

Product _____

Part 1	Part 2	Part 3	Part 4	Part 5

8

Conclusion

In writing *Business Aha! Tips…on Creativity*, we hoped to encourage creativity in your life and your work. Even more specifically, we wanted to help you create that Aha! Moment when inspiration leads to clear innovation for success. Let's review what we covered in the book.

Why is creativity important? As the ultimate renewable resource, creativity helps lead to remarkable changes in your life, work, community, and country. It has contributed to significant improvements in the standard of living in countries that have excelled in creating new patents, publications, products, and services.

What is creativity? Creativity is, at its most simple, doing things differently to boost performance and success – of a person, an organization, a community or country. It's not found in "only certain people," or places or countries; you can't hoard it or save it; you can't pass it on to someone else. Creativity can be misused by generating ideas to mask incompetencies or deliver foul intent. It comes from inside each person and can be tapped anytime and anyplace. You can enhance creativity through encouragement and a disciplined process, which means making it a habit – building creative thinking into your daily routine.

Who is involved in the creative process? Really, anyone can be creative at anytime, anywhere. But within organizations, creative entrepreneurs have the vision of what an organization can do to make it different, better, and more innovative. Creative leaders translate those visionary ideas and guide others to make it a reality. Creative team members turn the ideas into reality.

How can people and organizations encourage creativity? Aha! moments come when we question basic assumptions. For example, why do meetings have to be one hour long? Sometimes aha! moments come when we step away from the problem and make new connections that we haven't seen before. Insight can also occur when someone in an organization has an aha! moment and then replicates the idea to other organizations. Finally, aha! moments can also come from the collective force of a group working together and learning from each other.

Design thinking is an approach to tackling unstructured problems that encourages suspension of answers, collection of facts, and brainstorming before coming up with solutions. It provides a way to take extra time for creative processes to take hold.

Sometimes, all the encouragement just seems to fail and you hit a wall. What then? There are many ways to deal with the wall: push through the wall, tear it down, go around it, paint it, or ignore it.

Fantasies can be a source of innovation. Technology in science fiction movies could inspire new ideas and even new technologies. Fantasies of phantom competitors can also motivate ideas and better ways to perform. Even fantasies about a dream job can spur action to learn what it takes to do the job…and then do it.

Where can creativity occur? Creativity can come from unexpected places—within traditional organizations, on a dance floor, and heading out for a long weekend on the ski slopes. The laboratory is not the only place. Creative cities and campuses bring people together to innovate.

What are some great examples of creativity? Innovations have come in all types of industries from computers (Ebay) to paper (Post-It Notes), toiletries (Crest Spinbrush) to movies (Avatar). Two "creativity machines" exist that have generated and implemented numerous ideas. One, the public sector – DARPA -- has generated innovations ranging from GPS to integrated circuits and another in the private sector -- the Walt Disney Imagineers –created the Tower of Terror ride, the 765 foot water coaster ride called Aquaduck.

When will creativity end? Never. Yes, there have been products that have gone out of date or failed such as rotary dial phones, encyclopedias, and the Edsel. But with each failure, there is a silver lining: dial phones are museum items, old encyclopedic books can capture kids' imaginations, and Edsel clubs can be the rage.

The bottom line with creativity -- practice it, nurture it, do it. Experience the aha! moments as much as you can.

Use it Now!

Chapter 8 puts the content of the book altogether. Now it is your turn to put it altogether. You should use creativity to further your career and your personal life. This page is designed to have you think what you can do to make positive changes.

Work Life:

Why do you need to make a change?

What change should take place?

Who would be affected by the change?

Who can help you make the change?

When would the change take place?

Where would the change take place?

How can steps be taken to affect the change?

Personal Life:

Why do you need to make a change?

What change should take place?

Who would be affected by the change?

Who can help you make the change?

When would the change take place?

Where would the change take place?

How can steps be taken to affect the change?

References

1. National Science Board (2012). Science and Engineering Indicators. Retrieved September 6, 2012 from http://www.nsf.gov/statistics/seind12/.
2. Breem B. (2004, December 1). The 6 Myths of Creativity. Retrieved September 6, 2012 from, http://www.fastcompany.com/51559/6-myths-creativity.
3. Ibid.
4. Ibid.
5. Ibid.
6. Ibid.
7. Winsor, J. (2006). Spark: Be More Innovative Through Co-Creation. Chicago: Dearborn Trade Publications.
8. Ibid.
9. Ibid.
10. Ibid.
11. Ibid.
12. Bennis, W. and Biederman, P. (1997). *Organizing Genius*. New York: Basic Books.
13. Kay, J. (2011, October 11). Genius Can Change the World. Retrieved April 18, 2012 from http://www.ft.com/intl/cms/s/0/2e5708d8-f369-11e0-b98c-000144feab49a.html#axzz1sR935Mw9.
14. National Aeronautics and Space Administration. (2012) The Science of Star Trek Retrieved April 18, 2012 from http://www.nasa.gov/topics/technology/features/star_trek/html.

15. Reibstein, D. and Wittink, D. (Winter 2005). Competitive Responsiveness. *Marketing Science*, Volume 24, pp. 8-11.

16. Queen, D. (2006). Interview on February 2, 2006.

17. Polancy, T. (2005). *So You Want to Live in Hawaii.* Honolulu: Barefoot Publishing.

18. Kay (2011).

19. Ibid.

20. Funalso.net (2012).Crazy Innovations. Retrieved March 22, 2012 from http://www.funalso.net/miscellaneous/innovations-crazy/944.

21. Malone, Thomas (2004). *The Future of Work: How the New Order of Business Will Shape Your Organization, Your Management Style, and Your Life.* Boston: Harvard Business School Press.

22. Chesbrough, Henry (2011, Winter). The era of open innovation. In *Top 10 Lessons on the New Business of Innovation. MIT Sloan Management Review*, 35-41 Accessed April 19, 2012 at http://sloanreview.mit.edu/files/2011/06/INS0111-Top-Ten-Innovation.pdf#page=37.

23. Ibid.

24. Cookson, Clive (2008, October 20). Seer of Society's High Tech Future. *Financial Times.* Retrieved April 19, 2012 from http://www.ft.com/intl/cms/s/0/53b74a74-9e40-11dd-bdde-000077b07658.html#axzz1sR935Mw9.

25. Ibid.

26. Ibid.

27. Ibid.

28. Disney World (2011). *Walt Disney History Exhibit.* Orlando, Florida: Disneyworld.

29. Ibid.

30. Ibid.

31. Golden, F. (2010). Innovations from the Disney Dream Team. Retrieved March 15, 2012 from http://news.travel.aol.com/2010/10/15/innovations-from-disney-dream-team/.
32. DCLnews.com (2011). Disney Cruise Line—Cruise Industry "Firsts" and Innovations. Retrieved March 15, 2012 from http://dclnews.com/fact-sheets/2011/06/10/disney-cruise-line-cruise-industry-firsts-and-innovations/.
33. Camp, R. (2011). Idaho Ranked First in the Nation for Patents Per Capita Retrieved April 18, 2012 from http://commerce.idaho.gov/news/2011/09/idaho-ranked-first-in-the-nation-for-patents-per-capita.aspx.
34. Florida, R. (2002). The Rise of the Creative Class. Retrieved September 7, 2012 from http://www.washingtonmonthly.com/features/2001/0205.florida.html.
35. New York Times (1982) Traffic now tuned to Boston's Tunnel Radio. Accessed May 7, 2012 from http://www.nytimes.com/1982/08/01/us/traffic-now-tuned-to-boston-s-tunnel-radio.html.
36. Wikipedia.org (2012). Capsule Hotel. Accessed May 7, 2012 from http://en.wikipedia.org/wiki/Capsule_hotel.
37. Handler, Jessica (2011). Rotary Dial Phone. http://www.defunctmag.com/defunct/handler.html.

Additional Resources

Barood, James ed. (2011). *Entrepreneurship and Innovation: Global Insights From 24 Leaders,* Madison, N. J.: Rothman Institute of Entrepreneurship.

Cropley, David et. al. eds. (2010). *The Dark Side of Creativity.* Cambridge: Cambridge University Press.

Denning, Peter and Dunham, Robert (2010). *The Innovator's Way: Essential Practices for Successful Innovation.* Boston, MIT University Press.

Edwards, David (2008). *Artscience: Creativity in the Post-Google Generation.* Boston: Harvard University Press, 2008.

Govindarajan, Vijay and Trimble Chris (2010). *The Other Side of Innovation: Solving the Execution Challenge,* Boston: Harvard Business School Press.

Herbert, Anna (2010). *The Pedagogy of Creativity.* Oxford: Routledge.

Johnson, Steven (2010). *Where Good Ideas Come From: the Natural History of Innovation.* New York: Riverhead Books.

Kaufman, James and Sternberg, Robert eds. (2010). *The Cambridge Handbook of Creativity.* Cambridge: Cambridge University Press.

Kerr, Barbara ed. (2009). *Encyclopedia of Giftedness, Creativity, and Talent. Thousand Oaks, Cal.: Sage.*

Low, Albert (2008). *Conflict and Creativity at Work: Human Roots of Corporate Life.* Sussex: Sussex Academic Press.

Richards, Ruth ed. (2007). *Everyday Creativity and New Views of Human Nature: Psychological, Social, and Spiritual Perspectives*, New York: American Psychological Association.

Markman, Arthur and Wood, Kristin eds. (2009). *Tools for Innovation*, Oxford: Oxford University Press.

Napier, Nancy and Milsson Mikael (2008). *The Creative Discipline: Mastering the Art and Science of Innovation*, Westport, Ct.: Praeger.

Rickards, Tudor, Runco, Mark, and Moger, Susan eds. (2009). *The Routledge Companion to Creativity*. Oxford: Routledge.

Runco, Mark and Pritzker, Steven eds. (2011). *Encyclopedia of Creativity. (2nd ed). Maryland Heights, MO: Elsevier/Academic Press.*

Singer, Irving (2011). *Modes of creativity: philosophical perspectives*. Boston: MIT. 2011.

About the Authors

Gundars (Gundy) Kaupins
is Department Chair and Professor of Management at Boise State University. He has a Ph.D. in Human Resource Management from the University of Iowa and is certified as a Senior Professional in Human Resources (SPHR). His publications include over 300 articles in job evaluation, training and development, Baltic studies, and human resource ethics in journals such as the *Academy of Management Perspectives and International Journal of Technology* and *Human Interaction*.

Nancy K. Napier
has a Ph.D. from The Ohio State University, teaches management and directs the Centre for Creativity and Innovation at Boise State University. She has published widely in academic and practitioner journals. Her most recent books are *Insight: Encouraging Aha! Moments for Organizational Success* (ABC-CLIO) and *The Creative Discipline: Mastering the Art and Science of Innovation* (Praeger).

www.ingramcontent.com/pod-product-compliance
Lightning Source LLC
Chambersburg PA
CBHW071133280326
41935CB00010B/1209